THE OPIN

D1269707

DATE DUE

The Opinionmakers

By WILLIAM L. RIVERS

BEACON PRESS   BOSTON

FOR SARAH, GAIL, AND MARIANNE

Contents

The Opinionmakers Revisited

A Preface to this Paperback Edition

I ONCE BELONGED to that small, unhappy class of writers whose attitude toward their own work fluctuates wildly. It goes something like this: At the hot moment when a book is completed, their prose seems so golden that they wish Shakespeare were still around to provide the competition that would push them to even greater heights; as No. 2, he would have to try harder. A few weeks later, though, these writers begin to doubt. When they reread their books, blemishes and flaws appear. Still later, the blemishes have become blotches, the flaws great fissures, and more than a few of these authors begin to wish that it were possible to buy up the entire edition and burn it.

I was long a member of this class because, I think, so much of my work was Pre-Intentional. That is, I would finish writing a book or an essay before I got the idea for it.

In the case of *The Opinionmakers,* the idea came ten years before the manuscript was finally completed. When the book was published in hard covers in 1965, the reviewers were kind, and it won the Sigma Delta Chi Award for Distinguished Research in 1966. Now, a year after publication, I suppose that many who are mentioned in *The Opinionmakers* wish *they* could buy it up and burn it, but I nurture the hope that it will lead the long and happy life of the durable book, its pages yellowing gracefully through the decades.

This is not to say that I have had no second thoughts (a euphemism for "regrets"). In fact, except for the last of these pages, which will assess President Johnson and Vietnam, this introduction to the paperback edition may seem to consist of little else.

But that is one of the chief benefits of paperback editions; one who has second thoughts also has a second chance.

The most persistent of the second thoughts is a question: Why did I merely touch on the humorists of political journalism? Anyone who believes as I do that government — any government — needs to be opposed by a questioning journalism must wince at the heavy-handed way too many journalists go about it. The humorists are important, then, for deft criticism of officialdom. And there is another reason. If the late Edward Angly was right in his acid salute to Leo Rosten's pioneering study, "At last, someone has come along who takes the Washington correspondents as seriously as they take themselves," the more adroit humorists are a subtle rebuke to ponderous journalism.

Russell Baker *is* given a few sentences — too few — in *The Opinionmakers,* and some of the lighter musings of some of the heavier thinkers are sprinkled here and there. I am happy that I remembered to appreciate Baker, but it hardly seems possible that I could have written a whole book on political journalism without mentioning Art Buchwald and Art Hoppe.

Buchwald is an important figure in Washington, and not merely because his raggedly written satires puncture official pomposity and leaven the political discourse. They do this valuable work, but Buchwald is much more than a fun-and-games columnist. He is a caricaturist whose wild whimsies cloak the most incisive attacks on officialdom that are being written today. Like most caricaturists, Buchwald is least successful when he is merely funny. No one who reads his column regularly and separates the caricatures from the chaff can escape the suspicion that Buchwald is a savagely hostile man. Perhaps he was shown in the most revealing focus on a television panel program shortly after the assassination of President Kennedy. When the moderator appealed, "Why is everyone blaming Dallas for this when it could have happened in any other American city?" Buchwald responded acidly, "It didn't."

Art Hoppe's wit is as sharp as Buchwald's, he writes as winningly as Baker, and he has more provocative ideas than either of them. Unfortunately, Hoppe is a Washington columnist who happens to live in San Francisco. Even so, no one points up more incisively the absurd aspects of high policy. Hoppe's occasional forays into the federal city yield so many of his richest columns (which he usually describes as chapters in a forthcoming book entitled *Strange Native Customs in Washington and Other Savage Lands,* that it is clear that he belongs there. (Hoppe and another San Francisco columnist, Herb Caen — who is surely the best anecdotist in American journalism — should be persuaded to move to Washington. Baker, Buchwald, Hoppe, Caen — it seems doubtful that Washington reportage would be quite so self-conscious with all of them at work on the home ground of national politics.)

There are other, more sober journalists who should have been listed among the elitists. Some were not for understandable reasons. Clayton Fritchey has just become a columnist after years of serving Adlai Stevenson, but it is already clear that he is an influential force. Don Oberdorfer has returned to brighten and solidify the pages of the Knight Newspapers after working in the minefields of the *Saturday Evening Post* (which, after being published nearly forever for no discernible purpose, is slowly becoming a periodical of substance and value). James Perry of the *National Observer* seems to me to have developed his own pattern of reflective reportage only recently. And Joseph Kraft's columns have also improved markedly — certainly to the point that lesser men in government and journalism cannibalize them.

I doubt that I should be faulted, either, for having given *The New Republic* less than its current due. Although it seemed to take on some new life with the coming of the Kennedy Administration in 1960, it was scattershot; one never knew whether an issue would be a joy or junk. Now, with Andrew Kopkind and James Ridgeway showing how journalists should combine perceptive fact-gathering and sharp writing, *The New Republic* is a continuing joy.

If such omissions from the first edition of *The Opinionmakers* are understandable, some of the others are not — even to me. "Inside Report" by Rowland Evans, Jr., and Robert Novak was already an influential force. Edward P. Morgan, Richard Dudman and James Deakin of the St. Louis *Post-Dispatch,* Richard Harwood of the Louisville *Courier-Journal,* Philip Potter of the Baltimore *Sun,* Merriman Smith of UPI, Richard Strout of the *Christian Science Monitor* (whose writing in *The New Republic* is so startlingly different from his newspaper work, and equally valuable) — all are journalists of the first chop who effect the level of national reportage.

For a brief period, I entertained second thoughts about *Time* and about Drew Pearson. Hadn't *Time* mellowed since I judged it harshly? Shouldn't Pearson's fearless work on the Liberty Lobby exposé and on the case of Senator Thomas Dodd weigh heavily enough to produce a more positive judgment? On closer examination, no. *Time* still slashes venomously and unfairly — however provocatively — at those who seem to endanger its mission of spreading Christian capitalism. And Pearson's column is still a melange of the sharpest investigative reporting and absolute claptrap.

Conservatives have suggested that I should have covered more fully — and in a tone more to their liking — Senator Goldwater's troubles with the mass media in 1964. I did not because assessing that campaign is impossible. For example:

On May 24, 1964, Senator Goldwater answered a question about strategy in Vietnam over ABC television:

> Well, it is not as easy as it sounds, because these are not trails that are out in the open. I have been in these rain forests of Burma and South China. You are perfectly safe wandering through them as far as an enemy hurting you. There have been several suggestions made. I don't think we would use any of them. But defoliation of the forests by low-yield atomic weapons could well be done. When you remove the foliage, you remove the cover. The major supply lines, though, I think, would have to be interdicted where they leave Red China, which is the Red River Valley above North Vietnam, and there, according to my geography, it would not be a difficult task to destroy those basic routes.

The Associated Press promptly filed a story that began:

> Washington (AP) — Senator Barry Goldwater said yester-
> day that low-yield atomic weapons could be used to defoliate
> the forests along South Vietnam's border to expose the jungle
> supply lines of the Communist-led rebels.

When a furor developed over "trigger-happy Barry," he exploded. In a letter to James Reston of the New York *Times,* Goldwater held; "The Associated Press eliminated the key sentence,
'but one that will not be used,' and around the world went the
distorted story of my desire to use nuclear weapons on the Vietnamese."

Now one of the most revealing aspects is that Goldwater, who
had actually said, "I don't think we would use any of them," later
quoted himself as saying — and no doubt *remembered* himself as
saying — "but one that will not be used," a far more emphatic
negative. This is not a trick of memory that is likely to startle
a psychologist. When we talk loosely and later regret it, most of
us prefer to remember less damning words.

A question remains: Did the Associated Press treat Goldwater
unfairly in couching his ideas in the sentence quoted above? Some
AP men thought so. Certainly, some of the newspapers which
used the AP story published it under scare headlines. And yet it
is difficult to understand how an AP man listening to a Presidential
candidate speak — and at some length — about how we might
start a nuclear war could have reported the quotation much dif-
ferently. One might argue that the safer course would have been
to print the quotation verbatim and let every reader decide for
himself what Goldwater meant. Would reasonable men derive anything very distant from a belief that Goldwater thought low-yield
atomic weapons *could* be used?

Trying to derive what Goldwater meant from what he said
was the most frustrating task of political reporters in 1964. Charles
Mohr summarized the problem in an Esquire article which included
this:

One night before a large crowd in Portsmouth, he answered a question by saying that the Civil Rights Bill of 1964 could be used to destroy freedom of worship and to abolish private clubs. An articulate young Negro, the local secretary of the N.A.A.C.P., rose and said politely that the bill would do no such thing.

"You're right," said Barry cheerfully, "but it could be stretched that far."

Although he prided himself on honesty, he was one of the most inconsistent men I have ever known. When he began to sense danger, he would often slip sideways, and sometimes even backwards. At an early-morning press conference at Laconia he was asked whether he would campaign on a promise to lead the United States out of the United Nations if Communist China were admitted to the U.N.

"I would be inclined to do so," he said.

The wire service and network reporters were still phoning this story to their offices when Goldwater took off for the nearby town of Meredith. I wasn't on deadline so I tagged along. He made his appearance there on a curb in front of a tiny crowd. One man said, "My wife wants to know what you do about the United Nations."

Goldwater said earnestly: "We must stay in the United Nations, but we must work to improve it."

"You never opposed the U.N. then?" the man asked.

"No," said Goldwater.

A little later he appeared at the local high school and said that if China were admitted, "I think it blows the whole thing to pieces."

That evening at Colby Junior College for Women, he said, "I've never said let's get out of the U.N. I don't know how that rumor ever got started."

On still another occasion, he said that he didn't think the world was ready for an organization like the U.N.

As a reporter, I hardly knew how to deal with this kind of problem. I wanted to print Goldwater's opinion accurately, but what was his opinion?

It should not be surprising, then, that Goldwater's ragged rhetoric was occasionally misquoted and that reporters sometimes placed his ideas in a fuzzy focus.

The most haunting of the second thoughts have revolved around Lyndon Johnson. They sprang from Bernard Nossiter's perceptive review of *The Opinionmakers* in *Commentary*. For Nossiter saw quite clearly that although the thesis of the book holds that it is natural for all Presidents to manipulate public opinion, Johnson's manipulations are treated bitterly. Why?

At least part of the explanation is rooted in the fact that I lived in Texas for two years and in Washington for three. And the view from these perspectives — at least for a non-Texan — is grim. For although Johnson is able and intelligent, knowledgeable and persuasive, it seems to me that he also epitomizes those aspects of "politics" and "politicians" that have earned the lurking distaste of most Americans. In short, he is a pure political animal — which does not say that he works for the "art of the possible" but that he promotes anything that will work. And that which fails must be made to *seem* to work. It is doubtful that we have ever before had a President who was quite so oblivious to all questions of taste and morality.

The war in Vietnam is a fascinating case in point. As often happens, James Reston summarized the problem most acutely. In a column published in the New York *Times* in July, 1966, Reston wrote:

> The Johnson Administration may finally get over its agony in Vietnam — it may even achieve its military objective in the end — but it will probably never regain the confidence it has lost in its judgment and veracity.
>
> With the bombing of targets on the outskirts of Hanoi and Haiphong, it has now done almost everything it said or indicated it would not do except bomb China, and the end of this melancholy chapter in American history is not yet.
>
> The Johnson Administration said it was not seeking a military solution to the war, and it is now seeking precisely that. It said it was there merely to help a legitimate Government

defend itself, and it has ended up by supporting a military clique that is not a Government, is not legitimate, and is not really defending itself.

Even when allowances are made for the uncertainties and moral ambiguities of warfare, the guile of this Administration, exercised in the name of high and even noble principle, is hard to match. It was not going beyond the 17th Parallel in Vietnam but went beyond. It was merely going to respond to enemy attacks on its bases, but it went over to the offensive. It was not going to get involved in a major war on the Asian land mass but it did.

The President was not even faithful to his bad resolves: He said he would not negotiate, but then offered to do so, and spoiled that by refusing to negotiate with the major elements of the enemy he faces. He has not merely misled his enemies but his friends. His old colleagues in the Congress have not forgiven him yet for tricking them into support of a blank check defense of all of Southeast Asia under circumstances they could not possibly oppose. And even in this last adventure in Hanoi and Haiphong, we are told officially that the bombing of targets there is not an "escalation" of the war.

The result here is an atmosphere of uncertainty and suspicion. The hawks are as confused as the doves about what is coming next. There is now not a single major nation in the world that supports Mr. Johnson's latest adventure in Hanoi and Haiphong. Even Prime Minister Wilson of Britain, whose economic policy depends on Mr. Johnson's continued support of the pound sterling, felt obliged to make a public statement against the bombing.

This question of confidence in the good judgment and good faith of the United States Government is really more important than anything else. The specific arguments about bombing or not bombing the oil refineries are not vital. Honest men can obviously differ about the wisdom of the decision. Nevertheless, the fate of Vietnam or the United States does not hang on any of these specific arguments.

But a great deal does hang on whether the American people can trust the pronouncements of their Government, whether they can remain united on purposes they understand and respect, whether our allies believe Washington really wants a compromise settlement in Vietnam, or merely an enemy surrender on Washington's terms.

Mr. Johnson cannot restrain himself from attempting to answer such criticisms personally. At first, he directed his fire at newspapers, and especially columnists, and praised television for presenting graphic fact. But by the fall of 1966 it had become widely known among the Washington correspondents that the President was unhappy because of stark television coverage of the fighting in Vietnam. In October, he burst out during a press conference: "Those of us who sit here in Washington watch what three networks put on the air and what three men decide you can observe from Vietnam and all of the international incidents. When we read six or seven columnists and two or three or four newspapers, sometimes we don't get it firsthand, and sometimes there is a little personal equation that gets into it and sometimes personal opinions are substitutes for facts."

Many of the attacks have been subtler. Anthony Howard, Washington correspondent for the London *Observer,* has said, "I had not been in Washington a fortnight before I was drawn on one side by what is known here as a 'high source' and solemnly assured that Walter Lippmann was 'senile' — a diagnosis which those who have met Mr. Lippmann know to be totally absurd." As for Reston, Howard has written: "Go to any Washington dinner party and a moment arrives when the Administration spokesman will lean across the table and confide that 'as an old newspaperman' he finds nothing sadder than the decline in Scotty Reston's reputation."

Such pathetic efforts symbolize a wide-ranging program of persuasion that begins on the battlefront. As the New York *Times'* man in Saigon, Charles Mohr, has written: "A steady stream of misinformation about the war in Vietnam is reaching the American

public." This is not surprising. Some military officials who once
took pride in the Defense Information School, which trains military publicists, agree with cynical trainees who hold that the military
information slogan, "maximum disclosure with minimum delay,"
should now read, "minimum disclosure with maximum delay."

In the end, the question is not whether Lyndon Johnson will
go to any lengths to work his will. The affirmative is obvious. The
real question is how many others will be infected by his example.

Introduction

"In this and like communities, public sentiment is everything. With public sentiment, nothing can fail. Without it, nothing can succeed. Consequently, he who moulds public sentiment goes deeper than he who enacts statutes and pronounces decisions."

—ABRAHAM LINCOLN

THIS is a book about modern political journalism. More precisely, it is about the interplay of politics and the press (meaning all the mass media) in Washington today. It is about government officials using reporters—and reporters using government officials.

Most of all, though, this is a book about the foundations of American democracy, for the play of politics on the press and the press on politics is not an abstract game. The subtle struggle over political information has as its end the making of public opinion, and it has been continuingly significant for two centuries. Unfortunately, it is often resolved into a meaningless debate as to whether the Eisenhower Administration, the Kennedy Administration, or the Johnson Administration denied "The People's Right to Know" by managing the news. Nothing is quite so absurd as thinking of news control by government as a modern phenomenon. The focus may be sharper now, but the truth is that information policy has been at the very center of governing the United States from the beginning.

Patrick Henry set the terms of the historic debate. The government, he said, must keep from the press "such transactions as relate to military operations or affairs of great consequence, the immediate promulgation of which might defeat the interests of the community." The press must prevent officials from "covering with the veil of secrecy the common routine of business, for the liberties of the people never were, or never will be, secure when the transactions of their rulers may be concealed from them."

The great question has always been: Which are the affairs which might "defeat the interests of the community"? The writing of the Constitution was deemed to be one. The delegates to the Constitutional Convention straggled into Philadelphia in May of 1787—their deliberations began nearly two weeks late—but for all the desultory atmosphere they were agreed from the beginning that drafting a new form of government, or shoring up the old one, would be impossible if their speeches were published piecemeal and debated on every village square. They took a pledge of secrecy.

There seemed to be good reason for a secret convention. Had the masses of Americans been able to read of some of the more extreme proposals, the convention hall might have been a focus for rioting. Brilliant, ambitious, thoroughly aristocratic Alexander Hamilton, holding that the "rich and well-born" must be given their "distinct, permanent share in the government"; smooth Cotesworth Pinckney politely threatening the withdrawal of South Carolina if the majority carried through its plan to abolish the slave trade; endless compromising on the part of several delegates whose public posture was inflexible principle—all this went on behind bolted doors.

One day a delegate carelessly mislaid his copy of the proposals. It was found and turned over to George Washington, the President of the Convention. He seemed to ignore it, but as the meeting was adjourning for the day, Washington stated grimly: "Gentlemen, I am sorry to find that some one member of this body has been so neglectful of the secrets of the convention as to drop in the state house a copy of their proceedings, which by accident was picked up and delivered to me this morning. I must entreat gentlemen to be more careful, lest our transactions get into the News Papers and disturb the public response by premature speculations."

Until James Madison's notes were published decades later, few Americans had any real knowledge of what had occurred during the Constitutional Convention.

Other powerful leaders were as convinced as was Patrick Henry that the common routine of government business must be publicized. They believed that the survival of the new nation depended upon information that would, in Thomas Jefferson's phrase, "penetrate the whole mass of the people." Madison, the Father of the Constitution, wrote: "Knowledge will forever govern ignorance. And a people who mean to be their own governors must arm themselves with the power knowledge gives. A popular government without popular information or the means of acquiring it, is but a prologue to a farce, or a tragedy, or perhaps both." Jefferson, who wrote the Bill of Rights, valued information above the federal structure itself: "The basis of the government being the opinion of the people, the very first object should be to keep that right: and were it left to me to decide whether we should have a government without newspapers or newspapers without a government, I should not hesitate a moment to prefer the latter."

Clearly, the founders considered informing the people to be a function of democracy. But they carefully refrained from setting up an official information system. Instead, the informing function was turned over to the press. In effect, the press—privately owned, beyond official control—was incorporated into the machinery of democratic government.

Surely, some of the genius of the American idea flows from the fact that the apparatus of information was made an independent part of the continuing government in a way that insured its freedom from any particular administration. Officials from the first have had to adapt to the anomaly of an information system that is *of*, but not *in*, the government. This established a natural struggle between the men of the press and the men of the official government. It is no accident that the "strong Presidents" revered by many historians and political scientists—Washington, Jefferson, Jackson, Lincoln, Theodore Roosevelt, and Franklin Roosevelt—are also the Presidents who have most adroitly manipulated information. Much of the history of American government pivots on the use of the press as an instrument of political power.

While a member of President Washington's Cabinet, Jefferson led the opposition to Hamilton's Federalists, who had already established *The Gazette of the United States* at the new capital in Philadelphia. Eager to develop an editorial voice for Anti-Federalism,

Jefferson tried to enlist Philip Freneau, a talented journalist who had
become famous as "The Poet of the Revolution."

Freneau declined the first offer. Lamenting the rejection, Jefferson revealed in a letter to Madison how much favoritism he was
ready to bestow on an editor who would echo Jefferson's views: "I
should have given him the perusal of all my letters of foreign intelligence & all foreign newspapers; the publication of all proclamations
& other public notices within my department, & the printing of all
laws. . . ."

Later, the itch for a newspaper that would speak for him led
Jefferson to woo Freneau by letter again: "The clerkship for foreign
languages in my office is vacant; the salary, indeed, is very low, being
but two hundred and fifty dollars a year; but it also gives so little
to do as not to interfere with any other office one may chuse. . . ."

The sinecure lured Freneau. He established *The National Gazette*, which immediately became the loudest Anti-Federalist voice
and the most incisive critic of President Washington. The attacks
were "outrages on common decency," the President protested. He
questioned Jefferson closely regarding Freneau's reason for coming
to Philadelphia. Jefferson replied that he had lost his translating
clerk and had simply hired Freneau to replace him. "I cannot rec-
ollect," Jefferson told Washington, "whether it was at that time, or
afterwards, that I was told that he had a thought of setting up a
newspaper." In any case, Jefferson pointed out, he could control his
employee in the clerkship, but Freneau was a free agent in editing
The National Gazette.

Washington did not ask that Freneau be fired, but he could not
control his anger. Jefferson described a scene that developed during
a Cabinet meeting shortly after Freneau had published a scalding
satire:

> The President was much inflamed, got into one of those pas-
> sions when he cannot command himself, ran on much on the
> personal abuse which had been bestowed on him, defied any
> man on earth to produce one single act of his since he had been
> in the government which was not done on the purest motives,

that he had not repented but once the having slipped the moment of resigning the office, and that was every moment since, that *by God* he had rather be in his grave than in his present situation. That he had rather be on his farm than be emperor of the world and yet they were charging him with wanting to be king. That *that rascal Freneau* sent him three of his papers every day as if he thought he would become the distributor of his papers.

Jefferson seized the publicity initiative as soon as he became President-Elect in 1800. The Nation's Capital was being moved from Philadelphia to Washington, and Jefferson persuaded young Samuel Harrison Smith to set up his newspaper shop there by luring him with printing-contract patronage. It was a blatant exercise of news management, but there was reason for it. Jefferson was so vilified by the opposition press that he once suggested that editors categorize the contents of their papers under four chapters: Truths ("The first chapter would be very short"), Probabilities, Possibilities, and Lies.

The party press dominated political journalism from the beginning of the Jefferson Administration. The President had other favorites—he once wrote to William Duane, editor of the wild *Aurora*, asking for "an exact list of the prosecutions of a public nature against you, & over which I might have controul"—but Smith's *National Intelligencer* was the dominant source of Presidential news. It was an efficient system. There were no Presidential press conferences, and no Presidential interviews. Other editors were forced to rely for information on partisans like Smith.

Presidential control of information began to reach its zenith in 1829. President Andrew Jackson, who subscribed to twenty newspapers and dictated to almost as many, led "King Mob" to the Capital and elevated journalism to a visible force in government. Despite its power, the earlier status of journalism had been suggested by William Cullen Bryant: "Contempt is too harsh a word for it, perhaps, but it is far below respect." The image changed quickly. In the judgment of historian James Schouler, "Jackson was the first President who ruled the country by means of the newspaper press."

President Jackson surrounded himself with newspapermen,

among them Amos Kendall, an able Kentucky editor who became the leader of the "Kitchen Cabinet." One Congressman later said of him, "He was the President's thinking machine, his writing machine, aye, and his lying machine." Another newspaperman, Duff Green, had proved his friendship for Jackson during the Presidential campaign by fabricating a story that President and Mrs. Adams had had premarital relations. Jackson asked Green to "remove to Washington and become the organ of the party."

Green's *United States Telegraph* was the first Jacksonian organ, and for a time it served the President well. But Green developed a strong liking for the ambitious and magnetic John Calhoun. Administration leaders urged the President to replace Green. Always fiercely loyal, the President would not, but Kendall persuaded him to bring in Francis P. Blair to establish another Administration paper, the Washington *Globe*.

Jackson was never content to have only one organ grinding his tune. For a time, there were fifty-seven journalists on the government payroll, and both Green's *Telegraph* and Blair's *Globe* carried the Administration line. But it was soon apparent that Blair was to be *the* official spokesman. A rival editor described him as "one who must be believed when professing to act by *authority*." Only six weeks after the establishment of the *Globe*, there was no doubt that Jackson would be a candidate for re-election; Blair had written: "We are permitted to say that if it should be the will of the nation to call on the President to serve a second term in the Chief Magistracy, he will not decline the summons."

Blair visited the White House almost daily, usually bringing a jug of milk from his farm at nearby Silver Spring. He and Jackson would lounge and drink and discuss Administration policy and *Globe* strategy. They shared the direction of both. Back in his office, Blair would translate the President's ideas into fiery editorials. In the White House, an assistant who came to the President with a sticky problem was likely to be directed to "Take it to Bla'r" or "Give it to Frank Bla'r—he knows everything."

Anti-Jackson factions feared the cruel hook of Blair's satire. In time, they learned to fear his devious system for spreading the influence of his paper. Blair would write pro-Jackson essays and editorials, plant them in small rural newspapers, then reprint them in the *Globe* as "indications of public opinion."

Two events of 1860 marked the formal funeral of the party press. The Government Printing Office was established, all but destroying the printing-contract patronage that fed so many Washington newspapers—and President-Elect Lincoln arrived in the Capital. Lincoln listened civilly to several editors who tried to persuade him that their papers should be his official journal. Then he rejected all offers. It was altogether characteristic of his shrewd approach to shaping opinion through the press.

Lincoln refused to adopt an Administration organ because he saw that the Washington papers were impotent and because he realized that tying himself to one newspaper would restrict his dealings with others. He owed political debts to many a publisher, having used the press from the beginning of his political career—even working anonymously as a correspondent for the *Sangamo Journal* while serving in the Illinois Legislature.

He was deepest in debt to Joseph Medill of the Chicago *Tribune*. Their relationship dated back to 1854, when Lincoln appeared personally at the office of the *Tribune* to pay four dollars for a subscription. Medill met him then, and over the years came to think of him as a great man. When the debates with Stephen Douglas made Lincoln famous, Medill circulated through Congress a ringing letter endorsing Lincoln for President. He pushed his candidate so relentlessly in the *Tribune* that Lincoln himself was disturbed. "See here," he said to Medill, "you boys got me up a peg too high. How about the Vice Presidency—won't that do?" Medill was adamant: "Now it is the Presidency or nothing."

As one of the founders of the Republican Party and the publisher of its strongest newspaper, Medill was in a unique position to promote Lincoln. He persuaded other party leaders to hold the nominating convention in Chicago in 1860, then took over the pivotal arrangements himself. He distributed all the available spectator seats to Lincoln's supporters, then manipulated the delegate seating so that those who favored William H. Seward could not affect the votes of the undecided.

"It was the meanest trick I ever did in my life," Medill confessed later, with satisfaction. "New York was for Seward. . . . It followed that the New York delegates were seated at one end of the vast hall, with no state for a neighbor that was not hopelessly for Seward. At the other end of the hall, so far away that the voices of the Seward orators could scarcely be heard, was placed Pennsylvania (the most important doubtful state). Between Pennsylvania and New York were placed the Lincoln delegates from Illinois; also those of Indiana and New Jersey."

Medill himself sat with old friends in the Ohio delegation and tried to win them for Lincoln. At the end of the third ballot—but before the totals were announced—it was clear that Lincoln was still $3\frac{1}{2}$ votes short of the nomination. Medill coaxed an Ohioan: "If you throw Ohio to Lincoln, Salmon Chase can have anything he wants." Ohio switched four votes from Seward to Lincoln, and the nomination was in hand.

Medill and the *Tribune* were safely for Lincoln throughout his Presidency, but Lincoln had to work for the support of the other powerful publishers. He was especially sensitive to the criticism of the greatest editor of the day, Horace Greeley of the New York *Tribune*. Greeley was often critical; the President was usually conciliatory. For a time, the New York publisher had a secret inside line to the White House. The President would give information to Robert J. Walker, a special advisor in the Department of the Treasury, and Walker would pass it on to Greeley "for the use or guidance of the *Tribune*."

With such adroit news managers setting guidelines, it is not surprising that some of the twentieth century Presidents have been able to use the press.

Although it is useful to trace the effect of politics and politicians on the Washington correspondents, this is not the beginning and the end of imbalance and distortion in political journalism. Nor is it the beginning and the end of this book. After all, one must take account of the shaping and coloring suggested by the poet's cynical phrase: "Whose wine I drink, his song I sing." Is the work of the Washington correspondents influenced by the biases of their employers? For decades, the reflex answer has been, "Naturally." Without denying that some bend to the pressures of the home office, the chapters which deal with the lords of the mass media suggest that the effect may be more complex than the reflex response envisions.

Indeed, it is implied here that the notion that reporters are bent, folded, and mutilated between government officials on the one side and their employers on the other ignores the strongest influence of all: the reporter's own quirks, prejudices, and idiosyncrasies, which include a yearning to be among those who stand highest in the Washington press corps. As H. L. Mencken pointed out long ago, a man seeks the approval of those who know what he is trying to do and are expertly equipped to judge his doing of it.

Ultimately, then, the aim of this book is to draw a picture of the huge corps of Washington correspondents and to point up the influences—the elite of the corps, officialdom, bossdom—which shape the reports the American people hear, see, and read.

If readers who have never practiced political journalism are repelled by what may seem altogether too much applause for journalists, they can take comfort from the thought that the journalists themselves may consider this book a deep wound. In my view, the book both praises and damns. But to some Washington correspondents, total praise would not be half enough. One who has written much about the press corps has suggested that someone should perform surgery to determine whether journalists really are, as they seem to be, the thinnest-skinned humans.

It is nonetheless true that the ideas expressed here owe much to all of them. Some consciously sat for this portrait, submitting to long interviews and answering letters and questionnaires at length. Some revealed themselves unconsciously in their writings. The debt to three correspondents—Walter Lippmann, James Reston, and Ben Bagdikian—is especially heavy. They have written as wisely about the role of political journalism as they have acted it. One who has left the press corps for a White House position, Douglass Cater, has been more helpful than any other. I had an unusual opportunity, working in Washington for *The Reporter* under Cater, to appreciate how acutely he performed as reporter, editor, and critic of journalism.*

If there is any hesitancy in this book, if some correspondents are tapped only when flaying seems in order, it may be charged to my most depressing experience as a reporter in Washington. One night shortly before the 1960 election, I covered a curious political-religious convocation during which Senator Hugh Scott, a Pennsylvania Republican, claimed that Richard Nixon had, in effect, integrated a Missouri motel. Like most of the other correspondents, I was for Kennedy. I didn't believe Scott. After taking detailed notes on the many other aspects of the convocation, I returned to my office and telephoned the motel. Was it true, I asked the manager, that Nixon had refused to allow his campaign entourage to put up at the motel if the segregationist policy was not changed immediately? "Yes, that's true," the manager said, "and we're still integrated."

The next morning, I wrote this report on the convocation:

> The Republican campaign to convince Negro voters that Senator John Kennedy has two positions on civil rights—one for Northern audiences and another for listeners in the South—took some questionable turns recently at the national "Convocation of Faith" of the million-member African Methodist Episcopal Church. Announcing that the convocation was also "a platform for Christian statesmanship," Bishop James Madison Reid said that he had been rewarded when he asked the Republican National Committee to send over some "big timber" for

---

* The works of three political scientists—Leo Rosten, Bernard Cohen, and Dan Nimmo—have also been influential. Rosten, who is now editorial advisor to *Look* and a writer and speaker of the first consequence, studied the newspapermen of the Washington press corps thirty years ago. His *The Washington Correspondents*, published in 1937, was my original stimulus. In quite different ways, Cohen's and Nimmo's more restricted studies (*The Press and Foreign Policy* and *Newsgathering in Washington*) have contributed meaningfully to the understanding of political communication—and to this book.

the closing session. "This," he said, gesturing proudly toward Jackie Robinson and Senator Hugh Scott (R., Pennsylvania), "looks like big timber to me."

Bishop Reid had not asked the Democrats to supply corresponding timber. In fact, the Bishop himself—who credits former Ambassador Henry Cabot Lodge with bringing fourteen African nations into the United Nations and "sending Ralph Bunche to Africa"—delivered two strong speeches for the Republican ticket, then punctuated the other addresses with "Yes!" and "Amen!"

Robinson, whose standing was attested by the appreciative nods and murmurs that greeted his allusions to "Rickey" and "the Dodgers" and "Chock Full O'Nuts," was appealingly direct in explaining why he supports Vice President Nixon. He had been for Senator Hubert Humphrey, but when Humphrey failed to get the Democratic nomination, Robinson braced both of the nominees on civil rights. "Nixon looked me straight in the eye when he answered my questions. . . . Senator Kennedy looked at Chester Bowles."

Robinson also alluded to the fact that "Vice President Nixon went into Jackson, *Mississippi*, and spoke for civil rights." But it was left to Senator Scott to build most of the case against Kennedy. Announcing that he was going to "call the roll on Senator Kennedy's lack of courage"—and getting repeated urgings from Bishop Reid to "Call the roll!"—Scott devoted most of his speech to it. For nearly an hour Scott found new ways to say that "This Harvard college boy . . . this rich Ivy Leaguer who has lived high on the hog all his life . . . is vocal in the North and silent in the South. Senator Kennedy has never yet mentioned civil rights in the South."

Senator Scott probably reached a new low in church oratory when he said that "Kennedy has never even integrated a bathroom," but it is unlikely that anyone will want to debate that point with him. It is a matter of record, however, that Senator Kennedy has spoken out on civil rights in the South. In Greenville, North Carolina, he said, ". . . every American regardless of his race or religion is entitled to his constitutional rights." In Memphis: "I want to see an America which is free for everyone, which protects the constitutional rights of every American, which will serve as our own symbol, our own identification with the cause of freedom."

Perhaps most important, Senator Kennedy said in Jackson, Mississippi, in October, 1957: "I have no hesitancy in saying the same thing that I have said in my own city of Boston: that I have accepted the Supreme Court decision as the supreme law of the land." This had apparently escaped Senator Scott's convenient memory, for he told the Negro churchmen, "Senator Kennedy has very suddenly, since he became a candidate, developed an interest in your problems."

It was left to Republican Chairman Thruston Morton to supply the irony: On the day Scott rewrote the record, Morton made him a member of the Republican "Truth Squad."

The fact is, of course, that *my* memory was more convenient than Scott's. Nowhere did I point out that Richard Nixon integrated a motel, a fact which certainly would have helped win Negro votes to his cause. I did not omit this consciously. My prejudices did the work and I was unaware of it until, much later, I read about the phenomenon known as "selective perception."

And so I usually respond to critics of political reporting, "Did you ever try it?" And I am likely to answer one who charges that a reporter is biased with, "Who isn't?"

CHAPTER ONE

The Paradox of Power

"The bars, lounges, and dining tables of the National Press Club have been a kind of alchemist's retort in which thousands of Washington stories have been distilled, synthesized, or even induced out of the thin but susceptible air."

—CABELL PHILLIPS
of the New York *Times*

"Before anybody gets the chance to ask, I want to make clear that the remark about Sweden's high rates of suicide and alcoholism which I made in Chicago some years ago was based on what I had then recently read in an American magazine."

—President EISENHOWER,
speaking in Stockholm

IF instead of building the nation's Capital on the mudflats of the Potomac, we had set it down in the turbulent center of a great city— New York, or even Boston—our attitudes toward politics might be profoundly different. For one thing, imagining politicians and public servants jousting in an environment not given over entirely to government makes their isolated federal municipality seem limited and incestuous. But it is more to the point to visualize the national government as part of a complex city in which the literati and the social critics could not avoid rubbing elbows and shaking hands with officialdom. Politics might not be so peripheral and vague in the national literature, and social criticism might not be so divorced from political realities and so enveloped in conspiracy theories.

It is no accident that Richard Rovere has made this point most incisively. Rovere has a dual perspective because he commutes from his home in New York to Washington to write about national affairs for *The New Yorker*. He laments that "very few reflective, literary intelligences deal with public affairs in this country," and it is not difficult to explain this remoteness. For political man, no city is more exciting, more electric, than Washington. But for those with other passions, no city is so stultifying; the singularity of Washington's concerns creates an atmosphere of politics that is heavy and dank. None of the incisive minds who were honored during the Kennedy years of attempting to unite poetry and power lingered longer than it took to have dinner at the White House.

The result of intellectual estrangement has been the elevation of the journalist. In other world capitals—which, significantly, are part of the structure of cosmopolitan cities—he must vie with the novelist and the critic in analyzing and interpreting public affairs. In Washington, the journalist wins by default.

There is more to the pre-eminence of the journalist in American politics, of course—a function of a frenetic era. As James Reston has said: "A distracted people, busy with the fierce competitions of modern life, must be addressed while they are paying attention, which is usually at the moment of some great national or international event." The value of this insight is made clear by certain events of 1960 and 1961, when the people might have benefited from being less attentive.

On April 18, 1961, nearly six months after John F. Kennedy had defeated Richard Nixon for the Presidency, four social scientists from the University of Michigan held a press conference in Washington to present their analysis of the election. The analysts—Angus Campbell, Philip Converse, Warren Miller, and Donald Stokes— deserved a careful hearing. They had published earlier *The American Voter*, the most respected profile of the American electorate, and their study of the 1960 election was no mere scatter-shot sampling. Supported by a large grant from the Rockefeller Foundation, they had begun work in 1956 with a meticulous probing of opinion, and had ended with a round of depth interviewing *after* the 1960 election. During the Washington press conference, they announced their finddings and answered questions with confident precision.

Hadn't John Kennedy's Catholicism actually gained him more votes than it lost? No, the "Catholic issue" had cost Kennedy a million and a half votes.

Didn't Kennedy attract a great many Republican votes by his performance during the televised Great Debates? No, he lured *independent* voters by nearly two to one, but most partisan Democrats and Republicans responded favorably to their own candidates.

Moreover, the Michigan analysts reported, even though Democrats outnumber Republicans, Nixon had a clear majority among those who had made up their minds by the time the campaign began. But 36 per cent of the voters were still undecided. The great surge came during the last two weeks of the campaign, when Kennedy's closing rush carried along twice as many voters as Nixon's.

This is unquestionably the best analysis of the 1960 campaign: precise, scholarly, undergirded by months of careful research. In fact, there was only one thing wrong with it: By the time it was reported everybody knew all the answers—or thought they did. Political reporters had long before supplied ready-made conclusions for those who would accept them and raw facts for those who preferred to roll their own.

The conclusions were wildly varied, of course, but this was the consensus: Kennedy's religion may have cost him some Protestant Democrats, but it gained him even more Catholic Republicans; the cool Kennedy style had attracted many Republican votes during the Great Debates; Nixon had been coming on with a rush when Election Day arrived (an irresistible *non sequitur* that sprang from the late, cliff-hanging election returns).

In short, everybody knew a great many things that were not true.

A decisive majority will continue to nurture the unrefined conclusions of 1960, not the hard analysis that came along in 1961. The eventual seepage of scholarship—that intellectual osmosis through which we are gradually learning that Franklin Roosevelt was neither a saint nor a socialist and that Arthur Vandenberg was as much windbag as statesman—may publicize the scholarly election analysis in a decade or two. Until then, for most of us, it will not even exist. For by the time it was reported in April, 1961, *how* John Kennedy got elected seemed irrelevant; President Kennedy was sponsoring an invasion of Cuba, and the American people had turned to that. As Reston said, we must be addressed while we are paying attention.

More than any other event, a Presidential election reveals the influence of information, for the Presidential candidates, two men at the center of the world's attention, know little more about their fate than does the street sweeper with his television set in a fourth-floor walk-up. Neither candidate receives reports from election officials. In 1960, for example, scattered reports and projections came in from party professionals throughout the night, but their lack of validity is suggested by the one predicting at three o'clock on the morning after the election that Kennedy was on his way to a four-million-vote victory. For the facts, Kennedy and Nixon relied like everyone else on radio and television. And on the morning of November 9, twelve hours after the last polls had closed, Richard Nixon conceded. Electoral College balloting was six weeks off, and the formal Congressional canvass would not be held for two months.

Both the dominance and the subtlety of political journalism were apparent during the period that elapsed between Nixon's concession in November and the formal Congressional canvass of Electoral College ballots the following January. No one can really *know* who has been elected until Congress completes its canvass; yet everyone knew. Our immersion in the mass media is so total that we cannot focus on the truth—which is that until the meeting of the Electoral College nothing official can be reported. All anyone could be sure of was that newspapers, magazines, radio, and television were reporting a margin of slightly more than one hundred thousand votes for Kennedy.

When, at last, the time came for the canvass, Congress made the plodding finality of its own officialdom an occasion for humor, no doubt to cover the embarrassment of emphasizing the obvious. The Congressional review of Electoral College ballots was as relaxed as a lawn party. In his capacity as President of the Senate, Vice President Nixon opened the sealed certificate of the first state (alphabetically) Alabama, whose six unpledged electors had cast their ballots for Senator Harry F. Byrd of Virginia, and announced mock-seriously, "Senator Byrd is now leading." Byrd reddened, his fellow Senators laughed, and the most unknowing visitor could have guessed that the issue had been decided long ago. This was mere rigmarole.

Like the people they represent, government officials are attuned to the pace of the press.

Day-to-day government is no less affected by political journalism. McGeorge Bundy, one of President Johnson's chief assistants, says flatly that the federal establishment could not function without the Washington press corps, which means that journalism informs each of the many subgovernments of Washington about the activities of all the others.

How this works is suggested by the experiences of a young political scientist who joined a U.S. Senator's staff with the happy expectation that he would soon be immersed in inside truths. At first, that seemed to be the case; the Senate Office Building was awash in important and titillating information. Then the newcomer got settled, began to read the morning papers carefully, and discovered that his friends had been gathering most of their "inside" intelligence from the Washington *Post.*

It is true, of course, that Capitol Hill is an information center in its own right; individuals there have information that is never publicly reported. But in government as elsewhere, each worker is circumscribed, and his sphere is small. A Congressional assistant may spend much of one day absorbing the details of covert operations in Vietnam and learn much more than is published about the imminence of all-out war. But he hasn't the time to tell all his colleagues, and he is likely to know less about House debate that day than any tired tourist from Buffalo who wandered into the public gallery to give his feet a rest. And both must read the papers to find out what happened in the Senate.

Former Senator H. Alexander Smith of New Jersey has made it clear, too, that Members of Congress are not Olympians who learn everything in closed-door hearings and secret communiqués; they are also dependent on journalism. In an article for a journal of political science, Senator Smith listed thirteen different sources of information for Congress. But the mass media, he wrote, "are basic, and form the general groundwork upon which the Congressman builds his knowledge of current events. The other sources . . . are all supplements to these more basic media."

How hugely Members of Congress depend on the press was

illustrated by Senator Kenneth Keating of New York, whose re-election effort in 1964 was based in part on his reputation as a "Cuba expert." Late in the summer of 1962, Keating created a sensation in a Senate speech charging that 1,200 Russian troops were unloaded at the Cuban port of Mariel even as the Administration insisted that only Russian technicans were in Cuba. Senator Keating's information came to him from Nat Finney of the Buffalo *Evening News*. The publicity for this disclosure won Keating an invitation to appear on NBC's "Today." There he unveiled another sensation, reporting that 5,000 to 8,000 Russian soldiers were then in Cuba. This he had picked up from a story by Keith Morfett of the London *Daily Mail*. The Senator established his reputation as an intelligence expert securely in October with a speech holding that the Soviets were constructing missile-launching sites in Cuba—which was solid fact from a story by Hal Hendrix in the Miami *Daily News*.

The pattern is much the same throughout the Executive departments and agencies, even though some, like the far-flung State Department, have built intricate and wide-ranging reporting machinery of their own. In the field, according to one State Department official: "The embassies find out what the government to which they are accredited is doing via the press. . . . I used to mine the newspapers all the time for my reports to Washington." At the other end, officials are equally dependent on the press. One complained during a newspaper strike in New York that, without the *Times*, he couldn't keep up with what the State Department was doing. The importance of keeping up is emphasized by the occasion during the Kennedy Administration when the President called State and demanded an item-by-item explanation of the costs of one of Chester Bowles's foreign journeys. At the President's elbow was a clipping from the New York *Times* dealing with Bowles's expenditures during the mission.

Curiously, Dwight Eisenhower, who didn't care for journalists personally and preferred reading Luke Short to Walter Lippmann, summed up the influence of political journalism most concisely during a press conference ten months before the end of his second term. He had remarked earlier that he knew of ten or a dozen Republicans who could succeed him to his complete satisfaction. A reporter asked, "Do you think these, any of these twelve that you talked about, will emerge, surface, so to speak? Will you do anything to encourage them to emerge?" The President answered, "Well, I don't know anybody that can do the job better than you people here."

Naturally, the Washington press corps also has the trappings of power. Privileged as no other citizens are, the correspondents are listed in the *Congressional Directory;* they receive advance copies of speeches and announcements and read documents forbidden to high officials; quarters are set aside for them in all major government buildings, including the White House; special sections are reserved for their use in the House and Senate galleries and elsewhere in the Capitol. In all, fantastic quantities of government time and money are devoted to their needs, desires, and whims. There are White House correspondents who talk with President Johnson more often than do his own party leaders in the House and Senate; there are Capitol correspondents who see more of the Congressional leaders than do other Congressmen.

Everywhere, there are reminders of influence. The White House staff makes elaborate preparations for the correspondents to accompany the President wherever he goes. One macabre arrangement has the press plane always taking off after the Presidential plane and landing before it to provide the correspondents with a clear view of any catastrophe. The degree to which Congress caters to the press corps is suggested by this letter from ABC Correspondent Edward P. Morgan to the Sergeant at Arms of the United States Senate:

Dear Mr. Duke:
Since my election as Chairman of the Executive Committee of the Radio and Television Correspondents' Galleries, it has been brought to my attention the extreme need for a Fourth Assistant Superintendent in the Radio-Television Gallery.
The position of Fourth Assistant is essential in order that a staff member may be assigned to the Gallery facilities in the new Senate Office Building. We will be interviewing Senators on

radio programs (live and tape), television programs (live and film) in addition to the radio and television beepers to be assigned there.

Partial duties of the staff member to be assigned to the new Senate Office Building will be to answer the telephones and remain in the office prepared for any eventuality; help to arrange shows in the radio and television studios so that Senators will not be inconvenienced by having to wait for the completion of a film or recording; keep the working space, typewriters, paper, etc., in order so that radio and television correspondents can prepare their broadcasts.

Because of our increased workload, we find it impossible to assign one of the present staff to the new quarters. The present staff calls each committee daily for the following day's open hearings and/or executive meetings and witness lists; covers all open hearings; picks up releases and sees that radio, live and/or recording, television, live and/or filming, are arranged prior to the hearings and are supplied releases and needed information during the hearings. . . .

On the letter ran, piling up detail about the services provided by gallery employees and justifying the request for another. One fact is clear: those who man the Senate and House galleries—press, periodical, and photographers' galleries as well as those for radio and television correspondents—are paid by government but answer only nominally to government officials. They serve the correspondents.*

No wonder the Washington correspondents feel what one Presidential assistant has termed "an acute sense of involvement in the churning process that is government in America." A close view of

* Officials occasionally react violently to the correspondents' privileges. The late Congressman Clare Hoffmann of Michigan, always crusty, once retaliated against a reporter who had criticized the pay and privileges Congress has voted itself by shouting during a House session that the Washington correspondents "sponge" off the government. Later, he thought better of it and expunged his remarks from the *Congressional Record*. Similarly, Congressman Charles Gubser of California termed the correspondents "the worst freeloaders in the Capital." Under attack, he amended his judgment, saying that only a few could be described as the worst freeloaders.

the involvement of the American press corps so impressed Patrick O'Donovan, the perceptive correspondent for the London *Observer*, that he wrote: "It fulfills almost a constitutional function."

And yet, for an institution with great power, the press corps is the strangest paradox in Washington.

Paradox begins with the fact that almost anyone can enjoy a Washington correspondent's access to great men and events by saying that he is a correspondent. Admission to the President's press conferences and to the special Congressional galleries is controlled by identification cards, but more than one "free lancer" who was actually a lobbyist has slipped through. Although an outsider can seldom be certain when identification will be required, the correspondents' conferences with the mighty are sometimes open to anyone with the nerve to walk in. Moira O'Connor, a pretty Democrat, identified herself as a free-lance writer, climbed aboard the Goldwater campaign train, and cooly distributed a mass of newsletters ridiculing the Republican candidate before she was finally tracked down and thrown off the train.

The fact that correspondents are not licensed obscures the dimensions of the press corps. It is made up of seven hundred correspondents for wire services, newspapers, magazines, and radio and television stations and networks, nearly a hundred of them foreigners (like the correspondents for the Russian news agency Tass, who are admitted in exactly the same numbers—and suffer much the same travel restrictions—as American reporters in Moscow). Or it is twice that large if one counts newsletter employees, trade-press reporters (*Women's Wear Daily*, for example, maintains an alert Washington Bureau), photographers, television cameramen and radio technicians, and the round-trip reporters who come to the Capital on special assignments lasting days or weeks. Hundreds of reporters and editors for the many association publications issued from Washington are often on hand but are sniffily excluded—"Nine-tenths of them are out-and-out lobbyists," a correspondent maintains—but one probably *should* count the two-hundred-odd newsletter and trade-press reporters. Long disdained by the newspaper corps (which was the original Washington press corps and which has always passed lordly judgment on newcomers), they have become so numerous, and many are so expert and affluent, that they now receive fringe recognition. "Letter journalism," as the respected dean of the calling, W. M. Kiplinger, terms it, is thriving. Only the Government Printing Office has a higher total of annual mailings from Washington than Kiplinger's magazine and four newsletters. At the other end of a steadily widening spectrum is the one-man letter distributed by I. F. Stone, a tart-toned liberal whose appeal to his 20,000 subscribers was nicely defined by a fellow journalist: "I continue to read him because the wrong-headed, illogical, unfair and unjust way in which he writes about people I like is over-compensated by the precision, skill, neatness and dispatch with which he takes the hide off people I dislike."

To the extent that the press corps has any cohesion, it is stitched together by the two huge American wire services, Associated Press and United Press International. A few of the two hundred AP and UPI correspondents in Washington write thinkpieces—stories usually made up of a smattering of widely known fact, an indeterminate amount of inside information, and a dominating overlay of speculation. A few others have the leisure for investigation and reflection that is given to specialists and feature writers throughout the world of journalism. But most find themselves working at the pace described by one who quit as Chief Senate Correspondent for AP: "I was preparing about five thousand words of copy a day, and I filed most of it by telephone. If I got to think about a story at all, it was in the few steps running from a Senate hearing room to the phone booth." The average wire-service correspondent, in Douglass Cater's shrewd description, is "the bucket-boy for a never-ceasing stream of news that may be scooped up at any hour of the day or night and poured into print by the far-flung distributors. For him, the news is like fluid. It is capable of being bottled in any quantity."

The wire services have long tried to cover every major political event—with platoons at work on the great stories—and to man all the principal news outlets in Washington. The growing difficulty of that task is reflected in the reminiscence of a former AP bureau chief: "When I went to Washington I had seventeen men. When I left I had seventy-seven. And the whole time I was there, I was one man short."

Covering nearly everything means that some wire-service men are on the glamor beat, traveling with the President and hanging around the White House. This is actually one of the least-demanding assignments at times, a fact reflected in the long list of books written by White House correspondents during leisure periods. But when the President leaves the Potomac for the Pedernales, the general whirl is indicated by AP actions. One AP Washington reporter usually flies to Texas in the Presidential plane, another and an AP photographer travel in the press plane. AP men in Texas are alerted and start setting up shop—a plug-in phone, a telegraph printer, and a voluminous file on the President—in a hotel in Austin, which is 65 miles from the LBJ ranch. At the Stonewall Motel, which is a mile from the ranch, AP maintains accommodations complete with a darkroom where chemicals are already mixed for action. (Western Union often sets up a press room in Johnson City, 15 miles from the ranch, for all the correspondents.) Short-wave radios in the darkroom and in the photographers' cars and walkie-talkie units in the reporters' cars track the President wherever his unpredictable fancy leads him. AP has grown so wary of Johnson's wanderings that one Sunday morning when it was not known when, how, or whether the President would go to church, staffers covered all the ranch exits, Austin, Johnson City, and the nearby city of Fredericksburg. Mr. Johnson is not one to make the reporters' lives easier; he sometimes takes off in a helicopter bound for Austin after church while they try futilely to follow him by car.

Columnist Russell Baker suggests that the White House and the other beats imprint their personalities on correspondents: "The State Department reporter quickly learns to talk like a fuddy-duddy and to look grave, important, and inscrutable. The Capitol reporter eschews the raucous spirit of the White House and effects the hooded expression of the man privy to many important deals. Like the politicians he covers, he tends to garrulity, coarse jokes, and bourbon, and learns to hate reform. The Pentagon man always seems to have just come in off maneuvers."

Baker's half-joking judgment of the Pentagon corps of twenty-nine correspondents (thirty-odd others cover the Pentagon on occasion) seems close to the mark. One of them, Jules Witcover of the Newhouse National News Service, says of the breed, "By and large, the regulars see themselves as a squad of guerrilla fighters in a journalistic army of desk jockeys. They consider their beat to be tougher and more complex than any other, and they rate the department news policies under which they must function much more restrictive than those anywhere else in Washington." One reason for this abrasive attitude is suggested by one of their recent dialogues with Assistant Secretary Arthur Sylvester:

REPORTER: "Is Mr. McNamara investigating payments made by North American Aviation to Fred B. Black, a Washington representative of the company? These payments supposedly charged off against defense contracts?"

SYLVESTER: "Your question is a completely iffy question. I'm not aware (1) of any such payments or (2) they were charged off or what. So I don't know of any investigation being made. This is a matter before the committee, the Senate Committee. We're not getting into their business."

ANOTHER REPORTER (a few minutes later): "On Fred Black, you said you did not know of any investigation, is that right, that the secretary may be—"

SYLVESTER: "If I may respond to that without in any way reflecting on the man who asked the question, the question as it came to me was predicated on two *if*s and another *but*, neither of which I'm aware of. One, that there's some payments had been made and that there supposedly, was a word used, charged to something or somebody. I really haven't got a question to refer to."

SECOND REPORTER: "Well, I. . . ."

SYLVESTER: "And on the basis of that question phrased that way I said I was unaware of any investigation."

THIRD REPORTER: "Well, how would the question have to be phrased so that you would be aware of the investigation?"

SYLVESTER: "Well, I'm sure you're not going to ask me to ask myself?"

THIRD REPORTER: "Well, we can try that way. I mean, we're not doing very well the other way."

FOURTH REPORTER (still later): "Would you be glad to look into that one?"

SYLVESTER: "No, I wouldn't be *glad* to, but I'd. . . ."

FOURTH REPORTER: "There's now two kinds of investigation by you—those that you're glad to look into and those that you're not."

SYLVESTER: "I always look into them whether I'm glad or not."

In recent years, the Supreme Court, long a languid temple that was not so much covered as it was remembered on occasion, has been making pivotal news, thus widening the reporter's opportunity to make a contribution and a reputation. Before departing to take over the New York *Time*'s London Bureau, thoughtful Anthony Lewis took full advantage of the opportunity, and James Clayton of the Washington *Post* and Dana Bullen of the Washington *Star* were not far behind. But the wire services' passion for speed robs the able AP and UPI correspondents of a reflective role.

On decision days, Paul Yost of AP, who has been covering the Court for twenty years, and Charlotte Moulton of UPI, who has been at it for fifteen, don't even sit in the courtroom. They are one floor down in cubicles linked to the Court by pneumatic tubes which enable them to report the decisions to the world, rapid-fire, while the justices are delivering them. Other wire-service employees, on hand in the courtroom, stuff the printed opinions into the tubes as fast as they are distributed; Yost and Miss Moulton scan the opinions as they come down and fashion bulletins for teletype operators sitting nearby; the telegraphers transmit the bulletins by direct line to the AP and UPI bureaus downtown. By the time the Court delivers its last opinion, the first is probably on the air and in the headlines—sometimes misleadingly.

Yost and Miss Moulton spend many days getting ready for key

decisions—reading briefs (few of which are brief) and writing the background of pivotal cases in advance—but some decisions are cryptic and misleading. In a 1956 bus-segregation case, for instance, the Court order read: "No. 511 South Carolina Electric & Gas Company *v.* Flemming. Per curiam. The appeal is dismissed. Slaker *v.* O'Connor, 278 U.S. 188." Dismissal of the appeal seemed to outlaw bus segregation, with Slaker *v.* O'Connor, which had been decided in 1929, cited as a precedent. UPI duly reported that the Court had outlawed segregation on buses, and this was splashed on front pages everywhere. Actually, the opinion was not nearly so sweeping; the Supreme Court had merely refused to consider the appeal because the trial court had not reached a final judgment—which had also been true of Slaker *v.* O'Connor. The AP report was also wrong.

Drudgery of sorts is an element even on prestigious beats. "Delegation calling on Pentagon about military facility for Boise area; please cover," a UPI client newspaper requests, and a correspondent who may be exploring the higher reaches of defense policy must drop everything and try to divine which of the thirty thousand Pentagon employees the Idaho delegation is calling on. (With innocent self-concern, some editors assume that *everybody* is aware of home-town hopes and problems.) Similar vague requests reach most beats. Eager to keep their clients happy, and realizing that nothing in Washington is quite so important to Boise or Mineral Wells as decisions that affect a local situation, both AP and UPI follow through—even to the point, in one case, of reporting on the progress of a Texas Congressman's romance with his secretary (both of whom were, after all, "local" people). In some desperation, AP long ago set up its "Special Desk," now manned by four editors and about twenty reporters. They answer queries and tailor news reports for restricted geographic areas. Thus, one AP correspondent combs Washington for New York and New Jersey angles and another ferrets out facts of interest to Arkansas, Louisiana, Mississippi, and Tennessee.*

* Technically, AP is an association of "members"; UPI has "clients." But the distinction is somewhat misleading. In practice, AP and UPI serve their affiliated newspapers and radio stations around the world similarly—and spend more than $50 million a year doing it. With the British-based Reuters, they are

The wire services are almost alone in covering colorless news outlets like the Department of Agriculture, where a correspondent can develop a feeling of purpose and influence only by reminding himself how many people are affected by crop forecasts and price reports. On forecast and report days at Agriculture, the atmosphere is top secret. Press releases are placed face down beside a battery of telephones shortly before 3 P.M. The reporters toe a white line, side by side, then stride across it exactly at three, riffle through the pages and begin dictating rapidly. It is a demeaning kind of competition, but hundreds of traders are crowded around the news tickers on the floor of the Chicago Board of Trade and other big exchanges, eager for every figure.

So important are Department of Agriculture figures that on report days government forecasters are in "lockup"—isolated behind locked doors, barred windows, drawn blinds, and dead telephone lines. The forecasters must show a pass to enter the lockup area, and once in cannot get out until the reports have been released. James Reynolds of Dow Jones News Service, which also reports the figures, has described graphically how the news is released: "A minute or so before release time the head forecaster signals the guards to unlock a door at one end of the corridor. Tight-lipped, staring straight to the front, and escorted by a guard, he then marches about forty feet to the release room where reporters wait. The lockup ends only when the newsmen step across the white line at the word 'Go.' "

Similarly, Department of Justice antitrust actions and Federal Reserve Board decisions, either of which can jolt the financial community, emerge from a shroud of secrecy that would do credit to wartime troop movements. Antitrust stories usually begin to break with cryptic telephone calls from Justice Department press officers asking correspondents to stand by. (As in many other departments, the press officers call the "regulars" on the Justice beat, not the entire press corps.) The Federal Reserve Board traditionally alerts

the only services that cover the world without government subsidy. Agence France Presse (AFP), the French news agency, claims to be free of government, but one of its executives admits that the huge fees paid by government ministries for AFP's news report could be considered a "disguised subsidy."

financial reporters at four fifteen for decisions to be released promptly at four thirty.

By far the largest contingent of the Washington press corps is made up of correspondents for the nation's newspapers, but it is wildly heterogeneous. At the top are those Russell Baker of the New York *Times* calls "the Brahmans"—bureau chiefs and syndicated columnists who are so powerful that public officials are eager to have them "to tea or dinner or a weekend under sail." Next come the correspondents for the thirty-man staff of the *Times* and for other large bureaus, less sumptuous, maintained by a score of metropolitan dailies and chain papers. The larger bureaus report major events almost as though there were no wire services covering Washington. Others specialize in depth reporting, which is the mission of New-house National News Service. In 1962, Sam Newhouse began setting up a twenty-five-man bureau to serve his far-flung holdings. The St. Louis *Post-Dispatch*, the Louisville *Courier-Journal*, and a few other papers maintain small, crack bureaus that seldom find it difficult to surpass wire-service reports, some of which are superficial and many of which are bland denominators that will appeal to a diverse clientele. Writing for a wire service, one weary UPI man complained, "is like having a thousand mothers-in-law."

Some of the small bureaus consist of one man serving a single paper or several. Maintaining even one man in Washington may cost $25,000 a year. Two hundred "stringers" supply stories to a number of unrelated papers (a small-circulation daily can get part-time service for $250 a year and boast about its "Washington man"). The staunchest of the multiple-stringer operations is run by Bascom Timmons, who arrived in Washington in 1912 and now has a staff of fourteen and a newspaper clientele of twenty-five. Instead of dupli-cating wire-service coverage, the small-bureau men and the stringers search the crannies between major news items for stories of special interest to St. Petersburg and San Jose. Most of the Brahmans are sniffy about the "localizers" and delightedly pass on an apocryphal tale of one who was so intent on finding local angles for readers in Fort Wayne and South Bend that he rushed out to cover a Washington traffic accident because it happened on Indiana Avenue. There is an element of myopia in considering the local-angle reporters the peasantry. Ben Bagdikian, who was once a one-man bureau and now is one of the most respected magazine writers, points out that the localizers "serve the crucial function of telling the local citizen what the federal government is doing for and to him, and keep his distant representatives in Congress under a more or less steady spotlight."

The hundred-odd network correspondents and the more than two hundred magazine reporters and writers add another strain of incongruity. For although the mass media have generally taken on in news coverage the roles dictated by their differences, there are gridlike patches of overlapping and duplication. Like most of the wire-service men and many of the newspaper correspondents, radio and television reporters are primarily concerned with signalizing events—supplying the awakening alerts rather than fleshing out news in a context that gives it meaning. But they also work on documentaries, thus vying with magazine writers in fashioning reports that lend depth and flavor to events and personalities that have been previously shown only in silhouette.

Contrary to the stereotype of the journalist, most Washington correspondents are highly educated. Nearly 95 per cent attended college, and 82 per cent won degrees—figures that would be higher but for the lingering presence of veterans who date from the time when a reporter who had been to college was considered effete. (In contrast, a study of American business leaders reveals that only 76 per cent of them attended college, and only 57 per cent won degrees.) One in three correspondents have done graduate work, and one in five have graduate degrees. As Benjamin Bradlee, *Newsweek*'s Washington Bureau Chief, points out: "Nowadays, when a government expert gives a press briefing on news about economics, missiles, or Africa, there are four or five reporters in the room who know more about the subject than he does." One of the best of the newspaper correspondents, Ed Lahey of the Knight Newspapers, has only an eighth-grade education. And the best, James Reston of the *Times*, went to college, but, as a friend says, "It didn't take." It is safe to

say, though, that an applicant with an eighth-grade education
wouldn't be allowed to sharpen pencils in a Washington bureau
today.

Salaries, too, defy the stereotype. Although journalism has never
been noted for creating fortunes, the press corps is a reasonably
affluent society. It is not just that Drew Pearson, David Brinkley,
and a few other columnists and commentators make more money
than the President of the United States; nearly 10 per cent of the
correspondents are better paid than any other government official
except the President. The median salary for all correspondents is
$12,000 a year, and some double their incomes by lectures and free-
lance writing. The radio-television correspondents are the best paid
(a median of more than $15,000), followed by the correspondents
for magazines ($13,000), newspapers ($11,000), and wire services
($10,000).

There is paradox, too, in the nerve center of Washington journalism, the National Press Building, which has an atmosphere of
wisdom and wisecracks, significance and raucous informality (and
which some correspondents disdain as "taken over by the PR men").
It is a port of call for nearly every head of state in the Western world,
and many a pronunciamento has been made there. Khrushchev chose
to make his major address at the Press Club during his celebrated
tour of the United States. Also, and quite as typically, it has been per-
vaded by raillery. Two leading Congressmen of another era debated,
under Press Club auspices: "Whether Knock-knees or Bow-legs Are
a Greater Menace to Navigation." On another occasion, Congressmen engaged correspondents in a spelling bee—and won. President
Harding delighted in playing hearts there, and beleaguered Woodrow
Wilson said wistfully during one of his visits that if duty did not
prevent "I should often come to these rooms." The ambivalent tone
was probably best exemplified by President Harry Truman in 1948
when he awarded engraved silver membership cards in a solemn
ceremony, then ambled over to the bar, put his foot on the rail,
ordered up, and announced with a chuckle that the drinks were on
the National Treasury.

Dominating the corner of Fourteenth and F Streets in downtown

Washington, the Press Building is an awkward fourteen stories high in a city so distinctively horizontal that the building is sometimes called "the skyscraper." Located conveniently between the Capitol and the White House—a short three blocks from the latter—it is shabby functional, with a styling that one of the construction engineers termed "early Balaban and Katz." There is nearly always talk of major renovation, but the building never gets much more than a vague sprucing up here and there. Many of the one thousand offices are rented to lawyers and lobbyists, who are more concerned with tasteful appointments than are the correspondents. Few bureau offices are anything more than practical. For years the office of the Washington Editor of *The Reporter*—a magazine so significant that nearly every important government official either reads it himself or assigns it to an underling—was dominated by a cracked leather sofa and a desk which, lacking two legs, was propped at one end on a bookcase. Like journalism offices everywhere, those in the Press Building represent working space.

The activity in the corridors also indicates that journalists are about. Men slinging on coats and zipping up ties push through doors with the pressed, thoughtful air of someone going somewhere to do something important five minutes late. Fairly often, they are simply going upstairs; the Press Club occupies the top two floors, and the bar is usually open. Correspondents probably drink no more than do Foreign Service Officers or Senators, but the comment of one on a friend's removal from the White House beat is suggestive: "He drinks with absolute sincerity." Some of the offices of leading publications are housed elsewhere because of the alcoholic camaraderie of the Press Club. The New York *Times* Washington Bureau is several blocks away, a reporter explained, because the bar in the Press Building is a bit too convenient.

The Press Club is a suit-and-tie place, but it still has an atmosphere of informal beginnings. Established in 1908, its first home was over a downtown jewelry store. So many of the government great began to come in so regularly to escape and unbend that the correspondents moved to larger quarters over a drugstore. Women were excluded, but almost any friendly man with the money to buy his own drinks was granted associate membership. The Counsellor of the Turkish Embassy came in one night and was given a ten-day visitor's pass. When the pass expired, he continued to visit and spend freely, whereupon he was elected to associate membership "because of his intense interest in journalism."

The Press Building was constructed largely because the club needed new and larger quarters for all the visitors who dropped in and wouldn't leave, but also because James Bryan, a reporter-turned-promoter, needed a project. He had been working on a "Memorial to Motherhood," but the mothers began fighting among themselves. Bryan proposed that the correspondents put up a multi-million-dollar office building and reserve one floor for the club. It was a fantastic proposal (most of the correspondents were so casual about money that no member was allowed credit) and so it was done. In 1927, the building was completed and the Press Club was installed. Both have been in financial trouble ever since.

For a long time, the correspondents treated their club with the faintly suppressed cynicism of spit-on-the-floor police reporters— which most of them had been. They mocked their own pretensions, proposing Benito Mussolini for membership and forming other, subsidiary groups on improbable pretexts. The Castle Rock Survivors' Association was established on the spot when a Presidential campaign train hit a cow in Castle Rock, Wyoming. Like others whose work is built on words, the correspondents prize humor and verbal cleverness, approving the wry understatement of a notice that appeared on the bulletin board on January 23, 1961: "John F. Kennedy, a former newspaperman, now in politics, approved for non-active membership."

The press corps is now a bit more subdued. But the ingrained rough-diamond quality is still apparent—and nowhere so strongly as in reaction to one of their number who tries to smooth it over. Thus, when Joseph and Stewart Alsop published their deathly proud book *The Reporter's Trade*, Patrick O'Donovan reviewed it derisively:

> If these instructions are ever observed, there are great changes coming in Washington. Reporters will be well-, even richly-

dressed sophisticates who dine often and fastidiously in the company of officials selected for their wisdom and wit and for the fact that they were all at school together. Press conferences will be left to agency men who need not conform to the new dispensation. The conferences will be visited only occasionally by an exquisite dropping in to see how the old boy is making out these days. Officials who do not speak up, clearly and frankly, in a mood of total recall, will be admonished from the other side of their desks in terms proper from headmasters to nasty little boys. If they persist, they will be destroyed. . . .

The permanence of the old attitudes is apparent in the masculinity of the Press Club. Women have not been—nor are they ever likely to be—admitted to membership. They are admitted, grudgingly, to the dining room in the evening but never to the library. After years of appeals to Presidents and Congressional leaders to bring pressure on the club, women correspondents were even more grudgingly granted the right to attend Press Club luncheons addressed by public officials. Until 1964, they were permitted only to slip in after lunch was served and cover speeches while looking down from the balcony.*

The men of the press corps try to keep it a man's world even when it is not. Thus ABC Correspondent John Scali's ultimate compliment for Frances Lewine of AP: "She's such a good reporter everyone forgets she's a woman." Other women correspondents respected by the men get similar tribute: Meg Greenfield of *The Reporter* is almost invariably "Greenfield"; Bonnie Angelo of Newhouse National News Service is "Angelo"; Columnist Doris Fleeson is "Fleeson." In contrast, the most widely known women correspondents, May Craig and Sarah McClendon, are simply "May Craig" and "Sarah McClendon." Either, a correspondent explained, "will push a President aside to get in a picture."

To their chagrin, the male correspondents find they are obliged to read the women's pages of the Washington *Post* and *Star;* many

* Characteristically, women correspondents reacted to their exclusion from Press Club membership by forming *two* clubs of their own.

social gatherings are politically significant. As Meg Greenfield has written: "When it comes to social notes the hard news often turns up in a subordinate clause or embedded in other data that could not conceivably be of interest to anyone but women. It is by way of commiserating with the senator's wife over the prospect of changing the children's schools that we learn of the senator's plan not to seek re-election. It is the regrettable cancellation of the party that is likely to inform us, in passing, that it was canceled because the ambassador's government seems about to fall." The society writers knew of the coolness between Eisenhower and Nixon long before most of the other correspondents caught on; the Nixons were hardly ever on the White House guest list. The flinty *doyenne* of Washington society columnists, Betty Beale of the *Star*, turns up important items with metronomic regularity. Her secrets are simple: She takes in five hundred parties a year, brushes by those who are on their way out or down, and asks anyone of importance brass-jacketed questions. It is difficult to say "No comment" to another guest.

The knottiest paradoxes of Washington correspondence are the fuzzy rules that govern it. Nearly everywhere in the world of journalism, an unwritten code dictates that during a social occasion a reporter is just another guest (except for those whose mission is to describe gowns, flower arrangements, and door prizes). Some correspondents observe the taboo at Washington parties. When an official talks freely about a matter of moment, reporters are likely to ask for an appointment to explore it formally (sometimes to their chagrin; more than one heavy-drinking office-holder has decided at a soberer time that his tongue must have been loose). One Washington editor instructs his staff: "If the reporter is at a private gathering because of his person and not because of his position or profession, politeness and decent social relations indicate that he must specifically ask the person who discloses the information whether it may be published, and under what conditions. He may choose to do it on the spot, or to call on the source at a later time, operating without ambiguity as a reporter, and not as a social contact." But the reporters who observe such protocols are outnumbered by those who make nearly every waking hour a working occasion.

In 1959, Correspondent Earl Mazo, whose book *Richard Nixon: A Political Biography* had just been published, fell into conversation about it with Chief Justice Earl Warren at a buffet supper in the home of another correspondent. They were in an alcove off the living room, and soon Warren, who detests Nixon, was heard to snap, "You are a damned liar!" Clark Mollenhoff of the Des Moines *Register and Tribune,* who was standing nearby, rushed into print with a report of the incident. Then other correspondents who had been among the guests published other accounts.

There are several fascinating sidelights to this incident, not the least of them the varying accounts showing that veteran reporters who were on the scene could not even agree as to what had happened. Was Warren angry, as some wrote, because of the way his own relations with Nixon were described in Mazo's book? Or did Warren mean that Mazo was lying in asserting that the book was not a campaign document for Nixon? Mazo holds to the latter notion, but he admits that he was never really certain what had excited the Chief Justice. Warren, a quick-flaring man whose temperature falls as rapidly as it rises, apologized to Mazo moments after exploding and will not now discuss it (perhaps because he admitted later to Mazo that he had not actually read the book at the time of their encounter).

There was an agreement among the correspondents present to write nothing about the incident (as *Time* reported)—or there was no such agreement (as Mollenhoff maintains). Warren shouted his exclamation (Mollenhoff's version)—or he spoke quietly (another correspondent who says that *he* heard Warren speaking in a "perfectly calm voice" asks derisively, "Did Justice Warren say everything twice, using the same analogies, once in fury and then calmly later on?"). Mazo is uncertain. He says that the Chief Justice may not have been actually shouting. . . .

As every psychology student knows, there is nothing unique about moments of stress working strange reactions in individual witnesses. So it may be that the most instructive point is not the wild diversity of the accounts but whether the incident should have been reported at all. Mollenhoff is positive: "I'm a newspaperman. I didn't need anybody to tell me I had a story, and I didn't conduct a poll among the other newsmen present to find out what I should do." One who *did* conduct a poll found only five correspondents who said that in Mollenhoff's place they would not have written a story; fifteen would have written it, social occasion or not. Given these reactions, President Johnson should not have been surprised when he sociably showed a group of correspondents his Texas holdings and the fact that he did so while driving rapidly and drinking beer at the same time got into the papers.

The Warren-Mazo incident does suggest one of the conventions of Washington journalism: Correspondents agree on occasion to withhold certain stories. The record of the majority is so clear that many a public official will unburden himself of almost anything to trusted correspondents. But another convention thoughtfully envisions broken agreements: As soon as forbidden information comes out, everyone is free to write. When Mollenhoff's story appeared, the correspondents who thought there had been an agreement began writing, and cursing.

There are also agreements to withhold information for a specified period, and these are usually observed. But communication among the correspondents is sometimes ragged. One night when President Eisenhower's press secretary, James Hagerty, spoke on a "background only" basis (his words could be attributed only to "a high Administration official"), Roscoe Drummond, then Washington Bureau Chief of the New York *Herald Tribune* as well as a syndicated columnist, and Lyle Wilson, then manager of the Washington Bureau of United Press, went home to bed without filing stories. They thought a twenty-four-hour moratorium, often in force on background briefings, was being observed that night. They were awakened hours later by frantic calls from their New York offices: The *Times* and the Associated Press were carrying stories on Hagerty's background briefing. The moratorium had not been in effect.

Such misunderstandings arise fairly often because even the most basic conventions of Washington correspondence are so varied. A few inexperienced correspondents, and many public officials, simply do not understand the most widely used terminology. "Off the record" means that the information is for the correspondent's general understanding and is not to be reported in any form. "Background only" means that information may be reported, but not attributed to its source. "Not for direct quotation" means that information may be reported and the source named, but the correspondent must paraphrase, using neither quotation marks nor the official's exact words. (An ancient convention, this was devised to enable Presidents and Secretaries of State to speak without fear that slips of the tongue would bring serious consequences.) Too often, officials who actually intend to offer information for "background only" will say, "This is off the record," or, "Don't quote me directly." Some who want to speak "off the record" say, "This is for background only," thinking that the correspondents will not report the information but will use it only for their background understanding of issues. On Capitol Hill, some Congressmen who have been around nearly forever occasionally use phrases unfamiliar to the younger correspondents. "This is neither *from* me nor *for* me" is intended to mean that the information may be reported but should not be attributed to the source or his friends. To many correspondents, it means nothing.

Alfred Friendly, the respected managing editor of the Washington *Post*, once wrote a long memorandum to clarify the most common terms for his staff. Widely read throughout the press corps, the memo gives reporters considerable latitude in applying the "off-the-record" convention. A correspondent may seek the same information from another source, Friendly wrote, provided that he does not indicate that he has heard the news. "If he accepts the off-the-record convention as to the information itself, he usually may use it upon its public disclosure somewhere else. . . . In a public meeting or gathering, open to all without specific invitation, any attempt by a speaker to put all or part of his remarks off the record may be firmly and blandly ignored as an absurdity." During the 1960 Presidential campaign, the Protestant preachers who were dubbed "the Peale Group" (after Norman Vincent Peale, one of their spokesmen) held

a press conference in Washington to explain their opposition to a
Catholic President. Nearly a hundred correspondents were on hand.
When one speaker prefaced his remarks with, "Now this is off the
record," they ignored the injunction.

Friendly's memo warned against the sometimes slippery practice of disclosing "off-the-record" and "background-only" information to other correspondents. Such disclosures are not uncommon,
in many cases because the correspondents simply enjoy talking politics and are proud of their inside information; at times because one
who is bound to secrecy feels that the news he has is too important
to be hidden and should be given to a correspondent who has not
been tied up by a promise. Shortly after taking office, Defense Secretary McNamara held an off-the-record briefing to announce that the
"missile gap" which Kennedy had made such an issue during his
Presidential campaign actually did not exist. Correspondents who
had not attended the briefing learned of it from those who had, and
promptly published it.

Most correspondents and all public officials are troubled by the
flexibility of the ground rules (not to mention what Friendly describes
as "deliberate misunderstandings"). But very few in either group
would do away with the rules, which serve both. McNamara's "off-
the-record" briefing, for example, was not at all a case of largesse
gone sour. With the correspondents writing stories based on a continuing belief in a missile gap, the Secretary of Defense was in a
sticky position. To announce in an open press conference that the
gap had magically disappeared when the Democrats took office
would have publicized the fact that part of the Democratic campaign
of 1960 had been based on a myth. McNamara went "off the record,"
hoping to inform the correspondents who were writing about defense
policy of the true situation and at the same time to avoid making a
public admission. The ploy would have worked had not the correspondents who were present arranged for others to publish it.

Much more often, officials with a touchy story to tell find it convenient to employ the "background only" convention, which pub-
licizes the facts while cloaking the source. It is especially useful to

be able to call trusted correspondents in for group "backgrounders" (sometimes with portions of the discussion "off the record") because all correspondents, including the Communists, may attend press conferences. The correspondents prefer being able to attribute information to an important person, but they are aware that public policy or personal vulnerability often makes it impossible for an official to speak openly. And so they sigh and quote still another "responsible Administration official," or "Northern Senator," or "unimpeachable source."

"The drab truth," Russell Baker once wrote gloomily, "is that, besides having the President call you up to say that he means to fire the Secretary of Something-or-Other, there are at least 3,000 other ways of gathering news in Washington, all relatively unexciting, some incredibly tedious."

Avoiding the tedium of Washington correspondence begins with by-passing the handouts that flow by the hundreds from federal departments and agencies, few of which do more than record the eminently forgettable. Peace Corps Director Sargent Shriver has pointed out, only half in jest, that it is easy to take advantage of the correspondents' antipathy for handouts: "Whenever anything newsworthy happens—applicants flunking out or being sent home, shotgun weddings, rapes, fights with the natives, anything—we send it right out in a mimeographed release. You'd be surprised how few of them get printed. Whenever a paper or a wire service sees a mimeographed release, they chuck it right in the wastebasket on the assumption that all we're looking for is another plug!" When knowledgeable correspondents need more than a fugitive fact or statistic, they also avoid going through the press-relations office—"the gateway to the obvious"—preferring to speak directly to policy officials. Homemade shorthand (unlike English journalists, few Americans can take stenographic notes) lightens the routine of covering speeches. Knowing an individual's habitual phrases helps. When Governor Rockefeller is to speak in Washington, the correspondents know that they will soon be writing "bomfog," which is short for the Governor's favorite, "the brotherhood of man under the fatherhood of God"; "moat," which stands for "mainstream of American thought"; and "goveclop," which means "government closest to the people."

But the basic techniques of Washington correspondence resist short-cutting. One must interview endlessly, attend press conferences and briefings, set up occasional background dinners with important officials, and develop an ability to create friction in high places, which Baker defines as "the art of rubbing two natural enemies together." The leading correspondents are adept at exploiting the rich antagonisms between Congress and the Administration, between one agency and another, between a politician who has power and one who is hungry for it.

For a few correspondents, the result of working diligently and imaginatively is that they have themselves become an elite group that shapes much of the work of the entire press corps.

CHAPTER TWO

The Influence of the Elite

"The quickest, easiest, most reliable way in town to get on top of a fast-breaking story is to ask the other reporters what's been going on. The amount of note-trading is simply prodigious. Some of the greatest information trading centers in Washington are the White House lobby, the State Department press room and the Senate Press Gallery. Forty-five minutes at the press table of the Senate Dining Room is recognized around town as the equivalent of a full day's leg work in the darkest recesses of Capitol Hill."

—RUSSELL BAKER

Excerpt from a letter to *The Reporter:*
"I reverently read and irreverently steal from every issue in my own research on the questions of the time."

—HOWARD K. SMITH

THERE was a time, and not so long ago, when the Washington correspondent could cherish a notion of himself, in Douglass Cater's apt phrase, as "the supreme individualist in the age of the organization man." Few can now have any such pretensions. For, ironically, even as the most influential correspondents have improved Washington journalism and enhanced the position and powers of the press corps, these same correspondents have unwittingly limited the scope of all the others. There are still some individualists who go their own way, unmindful of the tone set by the leaders, but public officials and correspondents themselves complain that the elite group of the press corps shape the broad outlines of political journalism for all. Columnist Robert Novak charges that many of his fellow correspondents exhibit "sheep instinct." What has happened to alter a highly individualistic profession is tied to a basic change in political reporting.

Nearly every field has opinion leaders whose influence colors the work of their contemporaries, but journalism was once largely immune. Until the early 1930's, the work of the average reporter was so structured that his writing was little affected by what others did. His job was to fashion a clear and concise straight news story, start-

ing with the who, what, when, and where of an event and proceeding
toward the end, placing factual details in descending order of interest
and importance. He was to hold a mirror up to an event to show its
surface. Explaining why it had occurred and brooding over what
should be done about it was left to the editorial writers and columnists.

Then came the New Deal, and suddenly straight news reporting
seemed inadequate. Some correspondents say they can fix on the
exact time when "the old journalism" failed: the day in 1933 when
the United States went off the gold standard. Vainly trying to report
that cataclysmic and baffling change, they appealed to the White
House, and a government economist was sent over to help. Then the
correspondents tried to explain the new facts of economic life to the
American people in the economic specialist's idiom, almost disastrously.

The gathering complexity of public affairs during the New Deal
days, and later when the Cold War began, made it increasingly difficult to confine reporting to the strait jacket of straight news. Reporting what a government official said, or what Congress did, was often
misleading; the facts didn't quite speak for themselves. The correspondents began then, somewhat hesitantly, to build the structure of
interpretative reporting (actually pioneered by foreign correspondents and a few columnists whose forte was explanation rather than
opinion). They began to emphasize *why* events occurred and what
they *meant*.

Interpretation did not arrive full-blown—its structure, in fact, is
still developing—and so many editors and reporters resisted so
fiercely that even today some of its proponents gingerly avoid the
term, preferring to call it "depth reporting." For a time, a debate
split the top level of the great Louisville *Courier-Journal*. Editor
Barry Bingham argued: "The need for interpretative reporting becomes more insistent week by week." At the same time, Executive
Editor James Pope attacked the interpreters, maintaining that, "by
definition, interpretation is subjective and means 'to translate, eluci-
date, construe . . . in the light of individual belief or interest. . . .'
Interpretation is the bright dream of the saintly seers who expound

and construe in the midst of the news." To Pope and the other opponents, interpretative reporting was simply an abandonment of objective journalism.

The most insistent advocate of interpretation, Lester Markel of the New York *Times*, attacked the notion that any form of reporting could really be defined as "objective," writing:

> The reporter, the most objective reporter, collects fifty facts. Out of the fifty he selects twelve to include in his story (there is such a thing as space limitation). Thus he discards thirty-eight. This is Judgment Number One.
>
> Then the reporter or editor decides which of the facts shall be the first paragraph of the story, thus emphasizing one fact above the other eleven. This is Judgment Number Two.
>
> Then the editor decides whether the story shall be placed on Page One or Page Twelve; on Page One it will command many times the attention it would on Page Twelve. This is Judgment Number Three.
>
> This so-called factual presentation is thus subjected to three judgments, all of them most humanly and most ungodly made.

The debate is sometimes no more than a question of explicit definition. Reporting exactly what a Presidential candidate said in Oregon is clearly straight news. But how does one classify a story that matches what the Presidential candidate said in Oregon against what he said in California and points out that he was emphasizing different aspects of his policy and his program in each state? The interpreters call this interpretation; advocates of straight news say that such matching is entirely consistent with the concept of objective reporting.

Actually, the fine distinctions matter little, for today's correspondents are carrying political reporting to a level that is clearly interpretative. The leading correspondents inquire around, dig in, think through—then explain that the candidate changed the pitch of his oratory in moving from one state to the other because his private polling organization had discovered that his anti-Communist

image was weak in California and advised him to play up in Los
Angeles the belligerence of his tone when last he faced the Soviet
Premier.

One of the sharpest interpreters, Karl Meyer of the Washington
Post, captured the omniscient tone of the most exaggerated interpretations in this spoof:

> WASHINGTON, Feb. 29—The feeling in this city is that the
> President has given a new twist to the tired formulas of foreign
> policy by his bold proposal to exchange the state of Alaska for
> the East German People's Republic.
>
> But despite the predictable outcry that has followed the Presi-
> dent's carefully worded statement, the move is neither so ruinous
> as opponents contend nor as inspired a masterstroke as the
> administration's publicists insist.
>
> There would be gains and losses for both sides. Although the
> area of freedom would be extended to East Germany, the swap
> would also mean that the Soviet Union would acquire bases
> near our defense perimeter, absorbing in the process the people
> of Alaska.
>
> To an objective observer, the controversy over the President's
> proposals clearly provides another melancholy example of how
> the methods of diplomacy lag so sadly behind the needs of the
> atomic age. Surely such complex negotiations might best be
> carried on quietly by skilled specialists. At the same time, the
> necessity for secrecy—and the failure to brief the press—has
> meant that the public has been caught unawares, and a contro-
> versy damaging to unity is likely to follow.

The extent to which interpretation pervades political reporting
today is indicated, ironically, by a memo designed to warn Associated Press reporters against it. AP and UPI are generally considered
the last bastions of straight news reporting and, in fact, much of
each news report filed is as straight as fallible humans can make it
(although UPI is proud of its role in the development of interpretation). AP General Manager Wes Gallagher sought to emphasize in

the memo that "the AP man is not a participant in the news. He is the recorder of it." But in spelling out the wire-service mission, Gallagher unwittingly revealed how far interpretation has penetrated the AP report, not to mention his own concept of reporting. He cited disapprovingly an AP story that began: "Few Latin American military leaders have won such quick support from the grassroots as the one led by Col. _____," and cautioned, "How could any reporter know this for a fact a day or two afterward? Nothing in the article gave specific support for the statement. It was just incomplete reporting." This surely suggests that AP reporters can make such judgments—and thus participate in the news—by waiting long enough and developing support for judgments they care to make. This is somewhat different from dispassionately holding a mirror up to an event.

Gallagher went further, citing with approval the work of James Marlow, a specialist in interpreting the decisions of the Supreme Court. Marlow, Gallagher wrote, "has read countless books on the subject and has accumulated over 100 reference books. When writing about the Court, he is in a position, therefore, to cite specific cases and instances to prove the point he wants to make." This is hardly reprehensible (and, in fact, Marlow is highly respected), but it is quite different from merely recording facts. Gallagher seems to be suggesting that the AP reporter is free to make points, not just make note of actions, provided he first develops some expertise.

Gallagher's memo had the tone of a warning that interpretation had just begun to creep into AP stories. In fact, the AP report has for a decade been colored by interpretative writing on occasion. On January 15, 1955, this story was widely reprinted by AP members:

> President Eisenhower at midterm is a changed man—a man
> of increasing political awareness, with a firmer grip on the prob-
> lems of world leadership. . . . He has devoted nearly half a
> century of service to his country. As soldier and as President he
> has carved for himself a secure niche in history, but now he hears
> an increasing volume of criticism, mainly from Democrats. . . .
> He evidences a determination to mold the GOP to the "progres-
> sive moderate" pattern he has designed for it. . . . In spite of

ups and downs his goals have remained unchanged—peace for a troubled world and a "dynamic progressive, forward-looking" program to lead America down a "middle road" to greater strength and prosperity. . . . The President still exposes that sweeping infectious grin in all directions but there appears in his eye a glint of steel that seems indicative of a new kind of Eisenhower. . . .

Most proponents of interpretation (or news analysis, as some prefer to call it) insist that it is not opinion. The interpretative reporter *explains* while those who produce opinion pieces, editorial writers and columnists, *advocate*. It is nonetheless obvious that the readers of some interpretative stories would have no trouble discerning the reporters' opinions. One such report began: "An unseemly session-end Congressional haggle has made Congress look ridiculous." Another, a report on a speech that had been delivered by a right-wing extremist, began: "Outside the night air was cool and refreshing. Inside it was stuffy and frightening." During the 1964 Presidential campaign, a report labeled "News Analysis" began:

Last Friday in Portland, way Down East in Maine, a ferret-faced woman in flat shoes and a wool coat almost down to her ankles stood at the fringe of an airport crowd of some 3,000 persons as the sun burned off the morning mists.

"That's right," she said, with a curt nod. Her response was triggered when Senator Barry Goldwater told the gathering that the Civil Rights Act of 1964, which may affect Down Easters less than any other group in the nation, cannot by itself solve the problems of racial unrest.

She turned to see if those around her agreed.

It was near sunset, three days later, on Monday evening, that a chubby farm woman in a sweater stood crushed almost breathless against the airport fence at Burlington, Vt. She looked up at the speaker's stand, giving back the fixed gaze of the President of the United States, Lyndon B. Johnson. He was extolling the virtues of the Rural Electrification Administration, which has brought electricity to countless Vermont farms.

"And you," he emphasized, aiming his index finger directly between her eyes, "don't want that repealed either, do you?"

The chubby woman managed enough breath to join a full-throated chorus: "No."

These vignettes represented the comparisons and the contrasts, at least as seen through the same pair of eyes. . . .

One thing is certain—President Johnson sought the crowds, had them and proved he could stimulate enthusiasm; Senator Goldwater did not gather them and did not seek them out—and proved that he was willing to stand or fall with his hard core of believers.

Sharply negative reactions to making such free-flowing judgments in the news columns have helped to keep Washington journalism from becoming overwhelmed by interpretation. It is now an amalgam of straight news stories, interpretative reports, and a great many stories that have elements of both forms. The trend, however, is clearly toward more interpretation. One correspondent said, "My instructions are not to write a story unless I can put into it at least some analysis and interpretation."

One can applaud interpretative reporting—surely the events of a dismayingly complex world must be explained as well as recorded— and yet be disturbed by some of its side effects. For what interpretation has done is to place a high premium on several varieties of expertise. Forty years ago, the demands of Washington journalism were so slight that a reporter who was competent anywhere could likely be as competent in Washington as the next man. Today, the best interpretation makes extravagant demands, requiring insight, intelligence, resourcefulness, energy, and especially a nice talent for getting close enough to a public official to discover hidden significances and at the same time avoid imprisonment in the official's perspective. Considering also the necessity to present complex matters in simple and graceful prose, it is no wonder that the worst fault of much of the Washington press corps is the tendency to play follow the leader.

Journalism has always fed on itself. In Washington, because a single correspondent cannot simultaneously roam the corridors of Capitol Hill, cover the White House, sit in the Supreme Court, conduct an interview in the State Department, and develop an insight into the complex workings of the Pentagon, correspondents have long leaned on each other for "fill-ins." But the limitations imposed by time and by the distressing distances of Washington geography are no longer as important as the correspondent's other limitations. Never has journalism fed on itself so subtly, and in so many ways, as it does in this new era of interpretative reporting. Let one diligent correspondent bring to light the hidden facts and develop an insight into them, and a hundred others are working with the same facts and the same insight the next day, perhaps altering them just enough for purposes of disguise. Let one turn a crisp phrase, and the less inventive correspondents are turning it again almost instantly.

At its least important level, the cannibalistic quality of political journalism takes the form of literary thievery. This happens every day, but it reached the ridiculous state when Columnist Victor Lasky damned John Kennedy by stealing the phrases with which Meg Greenfield had attacked Richard Nixon.

From Meg Greenfield's "The Prose of Richard M. Nixon" in *The Reporter*, September 29, 1960, Page 17:	From Victor Lasky's *J.F.K. The Man and the Myth*, published in 1963, Page 358:
The standard pattern of Nixon's prose goes something like this: statement of one side of the case (a), followed by a statement of the other side of the case (b). Although the bridge from (a) to (b) is usually the word "but," other familiar locutions such as "at the same time," "on the other hand," and "however" also enable him to take a position and warn against it at the same time.	The standard pattern of Kennedy's prose went something like this: statement of one side of the case (a), followed by a statement of the other side of the case (b). Although the bridge from (a) to (b) is usually the word "but," other familiar locutions such as "at the same time," "on the other hand," and "however" also enabled him to take a position and warn against it at the same time.

From Greenfield, Page 19:

> . . . in Nixon's prose the straw
> man emerges as more than a de-
> bating device: it is an innate fea-
> ture of his thinking.

From Lasky, Page 360:

> In Kennedy's prose . . . the straw
> man emerges as more than a debat-
> ing device: it is an innate feature
> of his thinking.

Almost as frequently, the correspondent who looks into history for a different perspective on a current problem finds that he is an unpaid researcher for everybody else. At the height of the managed-news controversy, Carleton Kent of the Chicago *Sun-Times* pointed out that George Washington had managed the news of the Constitutional Convention by rigidly preserving the secrecy of its deliberations and that Abraham Lincoln had withheld his Emancipation Proclamation until it could be issued at a psychological moment. Within days, anyone who followed the news with more than casual interest could have heard the same information on two network television programs and one network radio program. A search through some of the nation's leading newspapers turned up the same facts in fifteen. Not long after, a news magazine sketched the news-management issue, and the Washington and Lincoln episodes turned up once again.

Similarly, Arthur Rowse of the Washington *Post* dug into the case of the dangerous thalidomide pills, trying to judge whether a more alert press could have prevented some of the infant deformities. "The Thalidomide Story," which was published in *Nieman Reports*, was painstaking reporting—and so valuable that one columnist simply took it over, summarizing the highlights without credit. Rowse protested bitterly, whereupon the columnist printed a heavily veiled apology: "We made some remarks the other day about Senator Kefauver and the thalidomide tragedy and readers have written about it. About the best account is 'The Thalidomide Story' by Arthur Rowse of the Washington *Post*, in *Nieman Reports*."

These may seem to be only incidents that deserve a high place in any responsible survey of plagiarism. But there is much more to them. They bring into serious question the concept that sheer numbers of correspondents will assure that the truth will become known.

When a few cut the pattern for the majority, co-operative plagiarism is dangerous.

The danger becomes clear when a false report traces a path around the wide circuit of the press. The "answer" to the great question that lingered after the abortive Bay of Pigs invasion of April, 1961—Had President Kennedy promised U.S. air support to the invaders?—seemed to be "Yes." Some of the invaders told a reporter that air cover had been promised and withdrawn at the last minute. A friend of an editor was in Washington and fell into conversation with a man who identified himself as an Air Force pilot who had been called back after actually taking to the air to fly support for the invasion. The first stories qualified the statements—"according to one of the invaders"; "according to an Air Force pilot,"—but the correspondents who picked up the substance of these stories to use in their own were not nearly so careful about qualifying. The "facts" were soon being confirmed by sheer repetition.

Alarmed to see hearsay harden into fact, Attorney General Robert Kennedy tried to refute it by announcing that there had never even been a plan for U.S. air support. The President backed him up. The considerable persuasive powers of the Kennedys seemed close to winning the day.

At this point, Jack Gore of the Fort Lauderdale *News* stepped in and confused the issue. According to Gore, both the Attorney General and the President were lying. Gore wrote that he was certain U.S. planes had been promised because the President himself had admitted it at a meeting with Florida newspaper executives. Interviewing the others who attended the meeting confused the issue even more; some remembered the facts the way Gore stated them; some remembered no such thing. The truth came out more than two years after the invasion when *Life* (which can hardly be accused of serving as an apologist for the Kennedys) published a formerly classified government document of the invasion period, which read: "The President has stated that under no conditions will the U.S. intervene with any U.S. forces." It turned out that Gore had remembered discussing air cover with the President, but it was air cover provided by the Cuban refugees themselves.

What happens when a thoroughly interpretative report begins *its* travels is suggested by events of December 31, 1962, when President Kennedy held a two-hour background briefing for thirty-five correspondents. As analyzed by Ben Bagdikian in the *Columbia Journalism Review,* the confusion began when a correspondent asked the President whether he had been asserting a more positive policy of leadership in recent weeks. Kennedy replied:

> Well, I think we are more aware, probably, that we are going to incur at intervals people's displeasure. This is sort of a revolving cycle. At least I think the U.S. ought to be more aware of it, and I think too often in the past we have defined our leadership as an attempt to be rather well regarded in these countries [the Atlantic Alliance]. The fact is, you can't possibly carry out any policy without causing major frictions. . . . So I think what we have to do is be ready to accept a good deal more expressions of newspaper and governmental opposition to the United States in order to get something done than we perhaps have been willing to do in the past. I don't expect that the United States will be more beloved, but I would hope that we could get more done.

This was not an innocuous statement, and it did signal that the U.S. was likely to be firmer in its dealings with friendly governments, but the Associated Press reporter interpreted Mr. Kennedy's statement in stronger terms than the President had intended:

> President Kennedy intends to follow up his Cuban success by exerting stronger leadership over the West's Cold War policies—even at the risk of offending sensitive allies.

Correspondents who were not present at the briefing had two basic choices: the hard-hitting AP story or a milder interpretation transmitted by United Press International. The French and German news agencies and Reuters (which, with AP and UPI, is one of the three most powerful news services in the world) used the AP story.

Thus, this became almost instantly the Case of the Multiplying Mistake. As Bagdikian reported, Louis Heren, a Washington correspondent for the widely quoted *Times* of London, was on the point of basing his own story on the UPI report, which was all he had at hand. Then a correspondent for the British Broadcasting Corporation walked into Heren's office in the National Press Building and showed him a copy of the AP story. Heren switched to it and produced a story that his paper, usually characterized by understatement, headlined:

Tough Leadership Resolution by President Kennedy

The headline was understandably strong; a typical sentence in Heren's story ran: "The President has made known that he will pace the foreign stage like a young lion. . . ." Similarly strong reports appeared in other influential papers everywhere. *Le Monde* of Paris headed its version:

President Kennedy Has Decided to Direct the Western Alliance Without Worrying About Objections of the Allies

The press corps has become so specialized in recent years that influence sometimes depends upon individual expertise. Correspondents writing a story that has an economic angle are likely to lean heavily on the reports of Edwin L. Dale in the New York *Times* or Bernard Nossiter in the Washington *Post*. Many who find themselves needing foreign-policy orientation borrow from James Reston and Max Frankel of the *Times* or John Hightower of AP. The science angles in hundreds of different stories may reflect the work of specialists like John Finney of the *Times*, Howard Simons of the *Post*, and Bill Howard and Gene Bylinsky of Newhouse National News Service. Almost anyone writing on space will probably consult *Aviation Week;* anyone writing on Congress is likely to use *Congressional Quarterly;* anyone writing on education is likely to borrow from the work of Erwin Knoll of Newhouse National News Service; anyone writing a multi-faceted story is almost certain to comb the New York *Times*—all *Times*men are influential.

Trying to identify the opinion leaders among the generalists who cover the full range of government and politics is hazardous. Excluding, for a moment, the columnists, one can be sure, however, that these are leading figures: Bagdikian of the *Saturday Evening Post* and *Columbia Journalism Review;* Meg Greenfield of *The Reporter* (who, in the words of one correspondent, "looks like a little girl and writes like a stiletto"); Robert Donovan of the Los Angeles *Times;* Jim Lucas of Scripps-Howard Newspapers; Clark Mollenhoff of Cowles Publications; Robert Riggs of the Louisville *Courier-Journal;* Benjamin Bradlee of *Newsweek;* John Steele of *Time;* Alan Otten of the *Wall Street Journal;* Chalmers Roberts of the Washington *Post;* Mary McGrory of the Washington *Star;* Peter Lisagor of the Chicago *Daily News;* Tom Wicker of the New York *Times;* Richard Rovere of *The New Yorker;* and Warren Rogers of Hearst Newspapers. For reasons that will become clear, the list is heavy with liberals. Conservative correspondents like Willard Edwards of the Chicago *Tribune* can never count on leading much more than a coterie of like minds.

To isolate more precisely the elite of opinion leaders among publications, columnists, and commentators, the correspondents were asked to rate those they rely upon and consider fairest and most reliable. (Commentators are considered in Chapter 5.)

The first question ran: Which three newspapers (other than your own) do you rely upon most often in your work? Obviously, like most newspaper readers, Washington correspondents will use papers published where they live and work. This is especially true of Washington, whose unique business is the federal government, and the correspondents do read and rely heavily upon the bright, strongly interpretative *Post* and the solid, stodgy *Star*. The most striking aspect, however, is the dominance—continuing since Leo Rosten's study of the press corps in the 1930's—of the New York *Times*. Of the 273 correspondents who responded, 225 listed it, a tribute to the *Times*' whole-souled attention to national and international affairs.

CAPITAL REPORTERS' OPINIONS ON JOURNALISM

Newspapers read regularly
Number answering—110

	Per Cent
New York *Times*	90.0
Washington *Post*	83.6
Washington *Star*	78.1
Washington *Daily News*	68.1
New York *Herald Tribune*	65.4
Baltimore *Sun*	63.6
Washington *Herald**	51.8
Washington *Times**	34.5
Wall Street Journal	6.3
Chicago *Tribune*	4.5

Newspapers used in work
Number answering—257

	Per Cent
New York *Times*	87.5
Washington *Post*	69.6
Washington *Star*	47.1
Wall Street Journal	33.1
Baltimore *Sun*	13.7
New York *Herald Tribune*	9.7
Washington *News*	5.1
Christian Science Monitor	3.1
Journal of Commerce	1.9
The Guardian	1.6

Newspapers: fair, reliable
Number answering—99

	Per Cent
New York *Times*	89.9
Baltimore *Sun*	48.5
Christian Science Monitor	17.2
Scripps-Howard Newspapers	15.2
St. Louis *Post-Dispatch*	18.2
New York *Herald Tribune*	17.2
Washington *Star*	14.1
Kansas City *Star*	7.1
Washington *Post*	5.1
Philadelphia *Record**	5.1

Newspapers: fair, reliable
Number answering—247

	Per Cent
New York *Times*	90.7
Washington *Star*	33.2
Baltimore *Sun*	31.6
Christian Science Monitor	27.1
St. Louis *Post-Dispatch*	24.7
Wall Street Journal	17.8
Washington *Post*	15.4
New York *Herald Tribune*	6.5
Milwaukee *Journal*	4.9
Louisville *Courier-Journal*	4.5

Magazines read regularly
Number answering—97

	Per Cent
Time	58.7
The Nation	34.1
Harper's	34.1
Saturday Evening Post	34.1
*Collier's**	28.8
The New Republic	26.8
The New Yorker	24.7
The Atlantic Monthly	19.5
Fortune	18.5
Reader's Digest	16.4

Magazines used in work
Number answering—203

	Per Cent
Time	33.5
U.S. News & World Report	33.0
Newsweek	32.5
The Reporter	24.6
Government publications	11.3
Harper's	11.3
Business Week	10.8
The Economist	7.9
The New Republic	7.3
Fortune	4.4

Columnists: *fair*, *reliable* Number answering—77		Columnists: *fair*, *reliable* Number answering—242	
	Per Cent		Per Cent
Raymond Clapper*	32.5	Walter Lippmann	41.7
Paul Mallon*	16.9	Marquis Childs	8.3
Walter Lippmann	11.7	William S. White	6.2
Arthur Krock	9.1	James Reston	5.0
Robert S. Allen—Drew Pearson**		Roscoe Drummond	5.0
	6.5	Joseph Alsop	4.5
Heywood Broun*	6.5	Peter Edson	2.5
"What's the News" (*Wall Street Journal*)	3.9	David Lawrence	2.5
		James Marlow	2.1
John T. Flynn	2.6	None	11.2

* *deceased*
** *now have separate syndicated*
columns

Another dimension is shown in the answers to the second question: Which are the three fairest and most reliable newspapers? Again, the *Times* was dominant, but more significant are the shifts of position, with the Washington *Star*, the Baltimore *Sun*, the *Christian Science Monitor*, and the St. Louis *Post-Dispatch* all moving up.

Not surprisingly, the three general news magazines—*Time, U.S. News & World Report*, and *Newsweek*—rank at the top of the list of periodicals the correspondents rely upon. They appear every week and are made up largely of reports on national and international affairs. But even as a group they do not dominate this list as the *Times* dominates the newspaper list.

The reason for the comparatively slender reliance on the news magazines becomes clear from the judgments of their fairness and reliability. So many correspondents mentioned during interviews that the news magazines could not be trusted that they were split off from the other periodicals to determine which, if any, are considered trustworthy. The correspondents were asked to name the *one* news magazine they considered fairest and most reliable. It was a revealing exercise. Twenty-four per cent of the respondents failed to list any news magazine; 17 per cent wrote "none"; and some decorated the margins of the questionnaire with comments like "Are you kidding?"

and "No such animal." *Newsweek,* with seventy-five votes, led the list, followed by *U.S. News & World Report* with sixty-six. *Time,* which had been first on the "relied upon" list, received only nine votes for fairness and reliability.*

Many correspondents also balked at judging the fairness and reliability of the magazines of politics and opinion. Thirty-four per cent failed to list a magazine in that category, and nearly 15 per cent wrote "None." Considering the number writing, "These magazines deal in *opinion*" and "These aren't supposed to be objective," it is clear that many correspondents do not consider it possible for a magazine that emphasizes opinion to be fair and reliable. Those who did judge them favored *The Reporter,* which received ninety votes, followed by *The New Republic,* with nineteen. No other magazine was listed by more than seven correspondents.

A number of correspondents also consider it impossible for any writer who deals in opinion to be fair and reliable. Eleven per cent failed to list a newspaper columnist as fairest and most reliable, and nearly 10 per cent wrote in "None." Yet it is clear that Walter Lippmann stands highest among the columnists. He received 101 votes, and no other columnist was even close. Reston, who has equal if not superior standing, works as columnist, reporter, and editor, and, technically, is not a syndicated columnist.

The most ironic aspect of opinion leadership in the Washington press corps is that the elite newspaper, the *Times,* does not print the column of the outstanding elitist thinker, Lippmann.

* The differences in the two newspaper lists and the two magazine lists are odd, but the correspondents do not necessarily rely for *facts* on newspapers and magazines they do not trust. A correspondent may rely upon three newspapers and think well of their fairness and reliability, but decide that three others that he does not consider as useful rank ahead of them in fairness and reliability. Similarly, a correspondent may "rely upon" a news magazine without trusting it, using it primarily to provide leads to stories he can research and develop on his own.

CHAPTER THREE

The Influence of Walter Lippmann

"Lippmann was particularly influential on monetary issues. Thus, when Roosevelt was pondering the question of the gold standard in the spring of 1933, a Lippmann column arguing that 'a decision to maintain the gold parity of currency condemns the nation which makes that decision to the intolerable strain of falling prices' convinced the President that the gold standard would have to go. As Raymond Moley was departing for London and the World Economic Conference, Roosevelt sent him off with a quotation from Lippmann. . . . Later, Lippmann urged tolerance toward the gold-purchase program, and in the spring of 1934 his column provided the formula that broke the deadlock over the congressional demand for silver-purchase legislation."

—ARTHUR M. SCHLESINGER, JR.

"I remember talking to Sir Anthony Eden at Geneva. . . . I know that he was relieved, and was convinced that the issue was not so critical and desperate, after he had read one or two of Walter Lippmann's articles."

—IVERACH MC DONALD

"Lippmann's voice comes from above and not from below; it certainly could not be confused with the voice of the people, which is the politician's most immediate concern, but it commands attention nevertheless. It may not be correct to assume that on all or even on most occasions Lippmann is the tribune of the national community of thinking men, but it is never safe to assume that he isn't."

—HARRY ASHMORE

"His colleagues at home and abroad read Lippmann with unique fidelity and respect; he is their foremost clarifier of complicated issues, and their acknowledged master of the prose of interpretative journalism."

—ARTHUR KROCK

IN other countries where newspapers employ political columnists, their standing with government is usually low. Consequently, for a foreign reporter in Washington one of the most disconcerting experiences is to ask complicated questions of high government officials and be referred to the columns of Walter Lippmann for the clearest answers. Lippmann by no means parrots official policy, but he usually interprets it more lucidly and traces probable consequences more pointedly than the policy-makers themselves can—and he often suggests compelling alternatives. Patrick O'Donovan of the *London Observer* has written: "State Department spokesmen answering general questions in private quite often say, 'Have you read Lippmann on that?'"

Nothing could be more impressive; like all centers of foreign-policy formulation, the State Department is jealous of its power and sniffy about "outside experts." And, indeed, a few officials dismiss Lippmann as an ivory-tower thinker who can write clearly about foreign entanglements because he need not deal with their harsh practicalities. But high officials in any administration must always consider Lippmann's position, and many heed him. Joseph M. Jones has written of the decisive weeks leading up to the Marshall Plan proposal that Lippmann "had a powerful impact upon policy thinking. His proposal that the European countries be asked to get together and agree upon a common recovery program and present us with a consolidated deficit was, so far as this writer can discover, original." As O'Donovan points out: "He stands for cold reason in international affairs and his influence is vast."

American correspondents are no longer surprised by Lippmann's influence—he has been affecting the course of government for fifty years—and they could not ignore him even if they wanted to. As college students, most of them read textbooks that were heavy with quotations from Lippmann's writings, or listened to lecturers who echoed the judgment of Clinton Rossiter and James Lare in their introduction to *The Essential Lippmann:* "He is perhaps the most important political thinker of the twentieth century." In Washington, they can feel his effect without reading his column. As James Reston commented when Lippmann returned from a trip to Russia and Germany: "His reports were part of the common conversation of the Capital. Every embassy up and down Sixteenth Street and Massachusetts Avenue discussed them and reported them to their governments. Members of the Senate Foreign Relations Committee read them and questioned the Secretary of State on his points."

Part of Lippmann's influence on the other correspondents springs from his central place in the international dialogue. It is often said that foreign governments accredit their ambassadors formally to the President of the United States and by private letter to Walter Lippmann. Certainly, his stature abroad is as great as it is in the American intellectual community. It is widely believed that during the crisis over Cuba in October, 1962, Nikita Khrushchev took a cue from Lippmann's column, which suggested that Soviet missile bases in Cuba be traded for Western bases in Turkey. Khrushchev proposed exactly that the following day. It is known that during the Eisenhower Administration, when U.S. relations with Russia were ragged and danger loomed, Khrushchev sought a meeting with Lippmann. The atmosphere had become so tense that a ban on the travel of American journalists to Moscow was rescinded. Scores of journalists visited the Soviet Union, and their reports were splashily displayed. Overtures were made to Lippmann, but he resisted for months before deciding to go. A correspondent who knew of the invitation asked Lippmann why he had not taken advantage of the opportunity to be the first to interview Khrushchev. He answered, "I am not a reporter."

Ironically, Lippmann is not a reporter in the conventional sense. Being first with the news does not interest him, but his most direct and measurable influence on the Washington press corps comes from his writing. He conceives of his column, he once said, as an effort to keep contemporary events in such perspective that his readers will have no reason to be surprised when something of importance occurs. Thus, although he has no effect on news gathering, his impact on interpretative reporting is profound. Those correspondents who seek to establish the meaning of events usually look to Lippmann for a useful approach. In Reston's words: "He has given my generation of newspapermen a wider vision of our duty. He has shown us how to put the event of the day in its proper relationship to the history of yesterday and the dream of tomorrow."

It is not just that Lippmann takes the long view, and it is not only that his words seem to carry, in the phrase of another journalist, "the authority of the basic intentions of the American political system." What Lippmann does, in essence, is to bring to bear on the questions of the time a powerful mind, a simple style that is shapely rather than staccato, and an absolutely relentless concern for disciplined thought and language. Thus, during the 1964 Presidential campaign, when Senator Goldwater charged the Democrats with planning an economy in which "no one is permitted to fall below the average," Lippmann icily wrote that "there cannot be an 'average' if no one is below it." No doubt many another journalist who knows how an "average" is derived might have made the same point had he only thought to analyze Goldwater's words. Lippmann thought and analyzed. Similarly, Lippmann seems to have been pretty much alone in thinking through the central implication of Senator Goldwater's "extremism in defense of liberty is no vice." To justify this to General Eisenhower, the Senator told him, "The most extreme action you can take in defense of freedom is to go to war. When you led those troops across the channel into Normandy, you were being an extremist." According to all accounts, the point seemed to register with Eisenhower. But Lippmann wrote: "The crucial truth is that when General Eisenhower went to war, he was not a private individual. He was not a member of a private and secret society. . . . The essence of the matter is that to be an extremist is to encourage and condone the taking of the law into unauthorized private hands. It is in truth shocking that the Republican candidate for President is unconscious of this sovereign truth. For the distinction between private violence and public force is the central principle of a civilized society."

Such insights—and the influence they create—are wine for all the other correspondents. As the only American philosopher who has committed himself to journalism, Lippmann nourishes the Washington correspondent's concepts of his own role. Although Lippmann sometimes writes about news in the philosopher's tone, as though it were already history, he considers himself first of all a newspaperman. Speaking at the National Press Club on his seventieth birthday (an occasion that attracted more correspondents than had come to hear Khrushchev speak in the same room a short time before), Lippmann said: "If the country is to be governed with the consent of the governed, then the governed must arrive at opinions about what their governors want them to consent to. How do they do this? They do it by hearing on the radio and reading in the newspapers what the corps of correspondents tells them is going on in Washington and in the country at large and in the world. Here we perform an essential service . . . we do what every sovereign citizen is supposed to do, but has not the time or the interest to do for himself. This is our job. It is no mean calling, and we have a right to be proud of it and to be glad that it is our work."

Certainly, one of the great points of pride for the Washington press corps is that, of all the meaningful careers open to him, Walter Lippmann chose to become a journalist.

By the time he was four years old, in 1893, Walter Lippmann was already politically aware: President Grover Cleveland was to him "a sinister figure," and William Jennings Bryan was an "ogre from the West." Lippmann remembers, as a seven-year-old, "waiting for the election returns of 1896 with a beating heart."

According to his childhood friend Carl Binger, who met Lippmann in 1896 in Dr. Julius Sachs' School for Boys in New York, he was a wonder child in other ways: "I don't suppose he ever got less than an A on any examination in his life. This habit began in Miss Estvan's class in 1896 and continued until we graduated from Harvard in 1910. He could recite the names of the states and their capitals in less time than anyone in the class. He could point out where the Guadalquivir arose and emptied and also the Guadeloupe. He knew his French irregular verbs so well that our goateed teacher, M. Jean Pierre Auguste Porret, preened himself when his prodigy of a pupil recited. He could translate Ovid at sight, and all the efforts of Mr. Douglas to teach us Greek met with success with Walter only."

The only-child object of devoted parents and an adoring grandmother, Walter traveled abroad even as a child and had all the money he needed. He was vigorous, mixing intellectual talk about art and the theater with school-fraternity life, hockey, and basketball. With Binger, he edited the *Junior Record*, a slender sheet whose editorials invariably began, "We, the editors of the *Record*, sincerely believe . . ."

Lippmann's standing after a short time at Harvard is indicated by what happened on his visit to a meeting of the Western Club. John Reed, who was later to write *Ten Days That Shook the World*, leaped to his feet as Lippmann came in, bowed sweepingly, and cried, "Gentlemen, the future President of the United States!"

There was much more than exuberance in Reed's introduction. In the Harvard Class of 1910, that may have been the most brilliant in history—Reed, the poets Alan Seeger and T. S. Eliot, stage designer Robert Edmond Jones, columnist Heywood Broun, and author Conrad Aiken were among the many students who became famous—handsome, modest Walter Lippmann was the most glittering of all. Concentrating on courses in art, philosophy, languages, literature, and economics, he completed the four-year course in three years and excited the attention of some of the world's keenest minds. Graham Wallas, who was Lippmann's teacher in a discussion course, dedicated *The Great Society* to him. William James, a flame of a scholar, was so attracted by Lippmann's slashing assessment in *The Harvard Monthly* of a book justifying capitalism that he stalked into the student's room one evening and announced, "I'm William James. I liked that review."

Lippmann was a startlingly versatile and active student. A champion debater, he wrote for the *Harvard Advocate* and the *Boston Common*, served on the board of *The Harvard Monthly*, worked among underprivileged children, and became the first President of the Harvard Socialist Club. He was at the same time, according to Conrad Aiken, "the darling of English 12." And when Lippmann completed his degree, he was asked to stay on for a graduate year and assist the great George Santayana in teaching a course in his history of philosophy. Finally, when Lincoln Steffens, the greatest of the influential "muckrakers," came to Harvard to look for an assistant and asked the faculty to recommend the best mind that could express itself in writing, Lippmann was the clear choice.

Steffens had two reasons for hiring him. He needed a young man like Lippmann, "who understood the meaning of all he learned," to help investigate Wall Street. Steffens expected to be able to show that the "invisible government" he had found operating the states and cities of America had a counterpart in big business. Also, Steffens had bet the editors of *Everybody's Magazine* that he could take an intelligent college graduate and fashion him into an accomplished magazine writer in six months.

The investigation of Wall Street supported Steffens' beliefs. As Lippmann later wrote: "We found that the anatomy of Big Business was strikingly like that of Tammany Hall; the same pyramiding of influence, the same tendency of power to center on individuals who did not necessarily sit in the official seats, the same effort of·human organization to grow independently of legal arrangements."

And Steffens won his bet. He sent an article written by Lippmann through the editorial process at *Everybody's*, leaving off the name of the writer until the article was ready to go into the magazine. The line that was added then, "By Walter Lippmann," forced the editors to concede that Steffens was right. A few months later, Lippmann himself was made an associate editor of the magazine.

This was the start of a wildly varied and productive decade for Lippmann. Soon bored with muckraking and with *Everybody's*—his duties included acting as "first reader of manuscripts and the sorter-out of jokes for the funny column"—he left to work for the newly elected Socialist Mayor of Schenectady, George Lunn. Drawn to socialism since his student days (and always carefully distinguishing it from Marxism), Lippmann was excited by the prospect of putting his theories into practice. But he soon found that the Socialist politicians, whose "good will was abundant and intentions constructive," were so enveloped in the petty vexations of politics and administration that the exercise of power crowded out all speculations about what to do with it. Lippmann escaped to Maine and wrote *A Preface to Politics*, a perceptive statement of the political role of the man of ideas. This was followed the next year by an elaboration, *Drift and Mastery*, that rejected socialism as doctrinaire and sterile and called for men of "passionate ideas."

The two books excited so much intellectual attention that Lippmann was invited to join the staff of a projected magazine that would soon become a major political force, the *New Republic*. His years with it were, on the whole, triumphant, though he had detractors.

One critic held that Lippmann seemed to assume "the responsibility of finishing up the incomplete work of the Creator." John Reed's poetic tribute was distinctively left-handed:

> . . . Lippmann,—calm, inscrutable,
> Thinking and writing clearly, soundly, well;
> All snarls of falseness swiftly piercing through,
> His keen mind leaps lightning to the True;
> . . . .
> Our all unchallenged Chief! But . . . one
> Who builds a world, and leaves out all the fun,—
> Who dreams a pageant, gorgeous, infinite,
> And then leaves all the color out of it,—
> Who wants to make the human race and me,
> March to a geometric Q.E.D.

But Theodore Roosevelt probably summed up the major reaction of the intellectual world. Lippmann, he said in 1915, was "on the whole the most brilliant young man of his age in the United States."

Still wavering between journalism and politics, Lippmann went into government service in 1916. He did the preliminary work on President Woodrow Wilson's peace proposals and wrote, with Frank Cobb of the New York *World*, the official American interpretation of Wilson's famous Fourteen Points. Again, however, Lippmann became disenchanted with practical politics, and especially with Wilson's inability to hear "the inward mutterings of the age." Back he went to the *New Republic*.

The period of Lippmann's greatest contribution began in 1920, when he joined the New York *World* as an editorial writer and began to focus his powerful mind on the ultimate problem of democracy: informing mass opinion. In *Liberty and the News*, he moved from his earlier plea for "a common intellectual method" to the necessity for "a common area of valid fact." This was preliminary; two years later he had thought through his new concern and published his greatest book, *Public Opinion*. Its value is emphasized by Arthur Schlesinger, Jr.: "The stupefying mass of writing, both learned and popular, which has appeared on this subject in the last quarter-century has added surprisingly little to Lippmann's analysis; and none of it has had anything like his fertility of insight or elegance of expression."

Public Opinion begins with the peculiar matter-of-fact power that informs all of Lippmann's writing:

> There is an island in the ocean where in 1914 a few Englishmen, Frenchmen, and Germans lived. No cable reaches that island, and the British mail steamer comes but once in sixty days. In September it had not yet come, and the islanders were still talking about the latest newspaper which told about the approaching trial of Madame Caillaux for the shooting of Gaston Calmette. It was, therefore, with more than usual eagerness that the whole colony assembled on the quay in mid-September to hear from the captain what the verdict had been. They learned that for over six weeks now those of them who were English and those of them who were French had been fighting in behalf of the sanctity of treaties against those of them who were Germans. For six strange weeks they had acted as if they were friends, when in fact they were enemies.

From there, Lippmann went on to show how little the world as it really is conforms to the picture of the world that we carry in our heads. He defined our stereotypes:

> For the most part we do not see first, then define; we define first and then see. In the great blooming, buzzing confusion of the outer world we pick out what our culture has already defined for us, and we tend to perceive that which we have picked out in the form stereotyped. . . . That is why accounts of returning travellers are often an interesting tale of what the traveller carried abroad with him on his trip. If he carried chiefly his appetite, a zeal for tiled bathrooms, a conviction that the Pullman car is the acme of human comfort, and a belief that it

is proper to tip waiters, taxicab drivers, and barbers, but under no circumstances station agents and ushers, then his Odyssey will be replete with good meals and bad meals, bathing adventures, compartment-train escapades, and voracious demands for money.

The central problem for liberal democracy, as Lippmann saw it in *Public Opinion*, was working out a relationship between the "outsiders," who know little of government, and the "insiders" who make the decisions. "No electoral device, no manipulation of areas, no change in the system of property," he wrote, "goes to the root of the problem." The solution he envisioned was the eventual creation of "intelligence bureaus" that could sift and refine facts. Nothing like this prescription has come about, but recognizing the need for organized intelligence was the final determinant of his own career. Gone was his earlier indecision. He settled firmly into the editorial page of the *World*. With the death of Frank Cobb in 1923, Lippmann became editor.

The editorial page of the *World* had been bright and hard-hitting under Cobb; it glittered under Lippmann. His own editorials were scholarly, but they were also effective in attacking the Administrations of Harding, Coolidge, and Hoover and the financial policies so dear to the wealthy, and they were telling in their promotion of an international spirit. Until the *World* died in 1931, a victim of a complex of forces including the Depression, Lippmann presided over the greatest editorial page in the history of American journalism.

The most influential aspect of his career began then. Lippmann accepted an offer from the New York *Herald Tribune* to write an independent column of political opinion—the first of its kind. As Cabell Phillips points out, David Lawrence and a number of *his* imitators had been writing political columns for years, but they "had limited themselves rigorously to interpretations of the news, telling what it meant, not what they thought about it. . . . But when they saw the temple walls did not crack under Lippmann's heresy, they began to put opinion into their columns too."

Now, in his later years, Lippmann has the aura of an aging eagle. His walk is not quite tentative, but one can see only a trace of the strong bearing that identified him twenty years ago. He talks simply, authoritatively, and quietly, never raising his voice. He is likely to answer a question, and then in the manner of men who do not trust their hearing, say, "What? What?"

He lives serenely, as always, following his own prescription:

> Every man whose business it is to think knows that he must for part of the day create about himself a pool of silence. . . . So long as so many jobs are an endless, and, for the worker, an aimless routine, a kind of automatism using one set of muscles in one monotonous pattern, his whole life will tend toward an automatism in which nothing is particularly to be distinguished from anything else unless it is announced by a thunderclap. So long as he is physically imprisoned in crowds by day and even by night his attention will flicker and relax. It will not hold fast and define clearly where he is the victim of all sorts of pother, in a home which needs to be ventilated of its welter of drudgery, shrieking children, raucous assertions, indigestible food, bad air, and suffocating ornament.

Lippmann's own pool of silence is the quiet—and quietly orna-mented—second-floor study of his home, which looks out over the Washington Cathedral. On the days when his columns are due (twice a week in newspapers, once a fortnight in *Newsweek*), he sits at his desk at exactly nine o'clock in the morning and writes in a small, almost illegible script, for a little more than two hours. No noise is allowed in the house during this period. Then Lippmann reads his column into a Dictaphone, editing even as he sounds out the words: "It is clear, comma, that, comma. . . ." (He has a horror of inac-curacy. While working for the *World* he began writing punctuation marks in words rather than symbols to make certain that the linotype operator would make no mistake. Editors who publish his column have become so accustomed to his painstaking certainty that once, when a typist's error got through his checking system, many news-papers published it exactly as they had received it on the theory that Walter Lippmann doesn't make such mistakes.)

His assistants type and check the column, Lippmann reads it again and confers with his researcher, and, if changes are made, it is typed and checked again. By twelve thirty, three hours and a half after he started work, the column is ready to dispatch and Lippmann is dressing for lunch at the Metropolitan Club. Afterward, he drives back home and spends much of the afternoon reading or walking with his wife, Helen. In the evenings, they usually go out for dinner. Once a week, they give a dinner party that is likely to include high government officials and diplomats. Every spring, whatever the state of the world, the Lippmanns go north to their camp in Maine. (Once, when he stumbled during a walk on the beach, his wife called, "Walk, Walter, don't *think*.")

Lippmann's friend Joseph Harsch of NBC has observed: "If you ask Walter Lippmann how he is feeling, you will get a serious answer. Either he is very well, which he usually is, or something is not quite right, which will be explained briefly, impersonally, and accurately. One does not make idle conversation with Walter Lipp-mann." Once, a government official hypocritically congratulated Lippmann on an essay attacking a position taken by that very official. Lippmann looked at him and responded quietly, "You know and I know that you do not mean one word of what you have just said. Good day!" The social relations of the columnist and the official ended there.

But Lippmann is not the "refrigerated intellect" of his reputa-tion. "What do you love?" he was once asked by an inquisitive woman. "The living world," he replied without hesitation or embar-rassment. According to his friend Reston, Lippmann is "extremely sensitive, easily hurt." Under attack, he is restrained, but his response to an attack launched by Columnist Frank R. Kent indicates the tension of his restraint: "I shall not reply to Mr. Kent's personal comments because all that would come of that would be that I might lose a good friend in trying to win an unimportant argument."

Lippmann gives time and attention generously to writers and

students who express serious interest in his life and work—and prefaces each interview with a request that there be no "personal questions." He will not discuss his first marriage, which began in 1917 and ended in divorce in 1937. But he will talk about anything he has written and is cheerful about his errors. Asked about an essay of long ago, he exclaimed, "Did *I* write that?" and shook his head and smiled at his own mistaken judgment.

Lippmann was pressed for time on two occasions when I talked with him. He was packing for the annual trip to Maine in the spring of 1959, but cleared away an hour when I asked for an interview. On the second occasion, in 1963, he invited me to his club when I asked to talk with him about changes in American journalism.

The evolution of political reporting has long fascinated Lippmann. He wrote more than four decades ago: "It is altogether unthinkable that a society like ours should remain forever dependent on untrained accidental witnesses. . . . The better course is to send out into reporting a generation of men who will, by sheer superiority, drive the incompetents out of the business."

Today, he thinks most of the incompetents have been set adrift: "Political journalism has grown enormously. When I started going to Presidential press conferences they were nothing but a gathering of people. Now they're a big show. The change of scale makes a great difference. There was a lot of give and take between the reporters and the President before, and that was good; but the reporters never did much thinking. The correspondents today are so much better. I used to be a freak in Washington because I had never been a police reporter, and a lot of the others didn't know what to make of me. But the reporters today *think*."

No doubt Lippmann's example has influenced much of the thought within the Washington press corps, but there is also an unfortunate aspect of his influence: the Lippmann Syndrome. At its most conscious, and harmless, it has some correspondents writing in longhand in the manner of the master. At a more serious pitch, it has them contributing hugely to the dreariness of much of our modern political journalism as they try to imitate Lippmann's style.

Like the novelists who hope to become Hemingways by rendering tales of conflict in simple prose, they are seduced by Lippmann's clarity; the result is a cluster of truisms. As Robert Massie has pointed out: "Lippmann is the kind of writer who drives to madness those who like to underline; first this sentence seems the key, then the next, and the next." The error of the imitator is in trying to put on this style as one puts on a coat. With Lippmann, the style is the man; lucid expression is the flesh of complex ideas that grow from sentence to sentence like a coral reef.

At its worst, the Lippmann Syndrome causes many another columnist to indulge himself in "thumb-sucking journalism"—the kind that comes from sitting, reading, and thinking instead of exploring the Capital for the views and events that make thoughtful journalism meaningful. Lippmann can do it successfully (although he often talks with high officials, and sits quietly in a back seat at press conferences, as well), but the odds against another possessing all of his privileges and qualities, not to mention his concerns, are unimaginably great. His indolent imitators, in the words of one correspondent, "are not interested in getting out into the vineyards and trampling up and down on the grapes to produce their wines."

They would do far better, one suspects, to pattern their research techniques on Lippmann's friend Reston, the most accomplished trampler in Washington.

CHAPTER FOUR

James Reston and the New York "Times"

"Perhaps the gentleman is reluctant to accept as conclusive proof the Navy's sailing directions or the word of a Navy admiral, but I am sure that he will admit that if you see it in the New York *Times*, then it is true."
—Congressman SAMUEL STRATTON in a House speech

"If the *Times* ran a piece about American policy toward Costa Rica, and it was all cockeyed and came from a postal clerk, it would still take at least an assistant secretary to convince the Costa Ricans it wasn't true."
—A State Department Official

"Reston gets up in the morning and thinks about what he is going to write that day. Next he sits down, writes it, and sends it off to his paper. After that, he goes over to the appropriate department and explains what he has written and how he expects them to conform to that day's story."
—A Washington Correspondent

REPORTER: Sir, do you mean that you are going to do today what the New York *Times* says you did in a private session yesterday?
OFFICIAL: I think it would be simpler if you just read Mr. Reston every morning, then we could avoid these briefings.

EVERY President of the United States, while he is in office, is the nation's most powerful man. However, as Oscar Wilde pointed out: "In America the President reigns for four years, but journalism rules forever and ever." This makes it necessary to take account of James Reston and the New York *Times*. Reston has none of the elegance of the first great *Times* Bureau Chief, Richard Oulahan, who carried a cane and had the hauteur that went with it. Reston lacks the imposing bulk and mien of his predecessor, Arthur Krock. A short, compact, energetic man, Reston looks pleasantly undistinguished and talks no more arrestingly than the average assistant professor of political science. But over the course of the past twenty years, partly in his own right and partly because he is the chief embodiment of the *Times* in the Nation's Capital, James Reston has probably been the most influential newsman in Washington.

There are many concrete ways to assess Reston's influence, but the most intriguing are the invisible. It is not possible to know how many policies have been quietly altered because Reston has questioned them, how many have never been instituted for fear that he would. One can only be certain that, in the area of the intangible, Reston is a looming presence. Joseph Kraft of *Harper's* has written: "On some big matters the State Department informs him almost automatically, as it would the representative of a major power."

One can find some of the tangible marks that Reston has left on every modern administration. Toward the end of the Roosevelt Presidency, he persuaded Senator Arthur Vandenberg (later known as "the father of NATO") to cast off the last vestiges of isolationism, then wrote the main parts of the famous speech with which Vandenberg rallied the beginnings of bipartisanship in collective security. During the Truman Administration, he probed so tellingly into the policy-forming apparatus of the State Department that Secretary Dean Acheson eventually stopped seeing his friend Reston on the sensible ground that he "might get the combination to the safe." In the Eisenhower Era, Reston swayed Secretary of State John Foster Dulles; some State Department functionaries grew to assume that Reston's writings were State policy. His impact became so pronounced that Eisenhower himself once exploded: "Who does Scotty Reston think he is, telling me how to run the country!" President Kennedy, knowing quite well who Reston was, asked him in for interviews and sought his support. When Kennedy attacked the steel czars in 1962, Reston reminded his readers in a light-edged column that a year had passed since the unhappy invasion at the Bay of Pigs, making it about time for another Kennedy crisis. Nervous over public reaction, the President shouted irritably upon reading Reston's column, "Doesn't he know I need his help with this?" President Johnson has courted Reston openly, once sending his private plane to transport the Restons to the LBJ Ranch. During the Democratic Convention of 1964, correspondents trooped in to question Johnson about his selection of a Vice Presidential running mate and found Reston making interview notes while the President was dressing to go out.

Reston's direct impact on government is impressive, but his indirect influence is awesome. If he is not the complete reporter, his news-gathering techniques are a model for the press corps, which multiplies his effect many times. One correspondent for a rival publication confessed that he had visited the *Times* Bureau on three occasions during a short period, ostensibly to see a friend, actually to try to eavesdrop on Reston while he was employing his widely envied talent for pulling important facts out of officialdom over the telephone. That talent—a combination of cajolery, assertion of right, and bluffing—has caused Krock to call Reston "the best telephone man in the business."

Shrewd bluffing is an important aspect of Reston's reporting technique. It begins, according to Senator Paul Douglas of Illinois, with something like the idiot's explanation of how he found a lost blind horse: "I shut my eyes and asked myself where I'd go if I were a blind horse. I went and the horse was there." In Washington, news-gathering is no game for idiots. Reston plays it by trying to imagine what *should* be happening in the highest government councils. He gathers shreds of fact from his many sources, then confronts the relevant official with bland hints that the whole truth is known. One former press officer has said that in tracing a news leak "you'd always find some official who would tell you: 'Sure, I told that to Reston, but he knew it anyhow.' I'll bet that ninety per cent of the time Reston didn't know it anyhow."

Reston has also affected the language of reporting. It was he who defined government manipulation of events and disclosures as "managing the news." (The Republican charge that Kennedy and Johnson have been the "news managers" is somewhat ironic; Reston coined the term in 1955 to refer to certain practices of the Eisenhower Administration.) And many a Washington correspondent calls the source of his own best news leaks "my Chinaman"—which springs from the time in 1944 when Reston exploited the unhappiness of the Chinese at the Dumbarton Oaks Conference in a way that won him a Pulitzer Prize and an FBI investigation.

This feat offers a sharp insight into Reston's techniques. The conference, which brought together in Washington delegations from

Russia, Great Britain, China, and the United States, was closed to
reporters. On the theory that the most disgruntled delegation was
likely to be the most talkative, Reston persuaded the Chinese to turn
over to him copies of the preliminary policy statements that had been
drawn up by each nation. From August through November, he
scooped the world on the conference day after day. U.S. Under-
secretary of State Edward Stettinius complained to Arthur Sulzberger, then publisher of the *Times*, that Reston's revelations were
likely to end the wartime alliance. Sulzberger retorted: "If unity is
so weak among the great powers as to be shaken by a few factual
stories, then it won't stand up anyway." The FBI was set on Reston's
trail in a futile effort to plug the leak.

This is testimony to Reston's patience. It is common for a reporter who has a big news break to splash everything on the front
page immediately. Instead, Reston husbanded the papers he had
obtained from the Chinese and used each at the moment when it
was relevant to the great powers' discussion.

More important, Reston's Dumbarton Oaks Conference stories
reveal his ceaseless search for new sources and a persuasive approach
to them. Many a correspondent develops friendships with a set of
sources and taps them for story after story. When they cannot help,
he is likely to be forced to use only what officials give everybody.
Reston also has regular pipelines, but when they are closed off, as
in this case (most of his friends in the State Department refused to
discuss the momentous conference with him; one warily declined
even to see him), he searches out another. Choosing the Chinese was
shrewd; they were most likely to benefit from whatever changes his
reporting might bring.

Like many other reporters, Reston makes friends with some
officials. Unlike most, he is careful to maintain his independence.
He met regularly and privately with Secretary of State John Foster
Dulles, but he wrote in 1958: "If General Eisenhower had had a
theater commander in the war who lost as much influence among his
men and got into as much trouble as Secretary Dulles has in the
past five years, he would have fired him long ago." Reston was generally friendly to President Kennedy, but he saluted influence-ped-

dling in the Kennedy Administration with: "There is a mess in Washington again, and very little evidence that either the White House or Congress is going to do very much to clean it up."

Reston's independence is founded on his elevated concept of the modern reporter's importance. "The Nineteenth Century," he has written, "was the era of the novelist. The Twentieth is the era of the journalist." Some correspondents are often vaguely, and secretly, uneasy when they break a major policy story, knowing that their reports may have the effect of altering the course of high deliberations. Not Reston. He takes an activist stance. The reporter must move in, he says, while policies are still being debated. If he does not "submarine" and illuminate the dark corners of the political arena, policy will have become so hardened by the time officials make it public that nothing can be done to change it.

Reston approaches public officials armed with a conviction of the primacy of journalism and with the air of one who is about the public business. Once, during the Eisenhower Administration, having obtained from a foreign embassy in Washington the gist of a cable that had been received by the U.S. Department of State, he spent two hours trying to pry the rest of it out of Acting Secretary of State Herbert Hoover, Jr. The cable was classified, but Reston made it clear that he knew most of the contents. Hoover finally put in a call to the White House, told a Presidential aide what Reston knew, and got permission to declassify it. Instead of showing gratitude, Reston lectured Hoover: Had he released the cable voluntarily, "We would not have wasted so much of each other's valuable time. Furthermore, I would not have to ask about U.S. foreign policy in a foreign embassy." (The difference between this and Joseph Alsop's celebrated conclusion to an interview with another high official—"You have just wasted half an hour of my valuable time"—may not seem significant, but it suggests one of the differences in their styles.)

In this and other instances, Reston's example has stiffened the backbone of many a correspondent facing high officialdom.

Reston's detractors are fond of pointing out that he owes much of his strength to the *Times*. This is not a view that can be dismissed

as mere envy. Every member of the *Times* Washington Bureau can
rely heavily upon his paper. One has said: "In Washington I may
seldom see anyone I know personally when working on a story, but
because I'm from the *Times* they will give me things they would never
give to an unknown reporter from some other paper in this town.
They will give me things and open doors to me because I'm from the
Times."

The New York *Times* was a great newspaper before Reston
joined the staff and would remain great if he should leave, largely
because it maintains brilliant reporters everywhere: Pulitzer Prize
winners like Wallace Turner in the San Francisco Bureau and perceptive foreign correspondents like Tony Lukas in India. Their
chief pride is in covering the world as no other newspaper does.
Proud stories travel from bureau to bureau. One tells of a State
Department official who said, when he was asked whether he could
add anything to the *Times*' reports on a crucial development, "Heav-
ens, no! Where do you think we've been getting our information?"

This was no jest. One of the most striking features of almost any
government office is a copy of the *Times*. Most high officials have
experienced the irritation of being briefed on developments by assistants who got most of their information from the same issue of the
Times that the official himself had read a short time earlier. For
governments here and abroad, the *Times* is the one indispensable
newspaper.

The omnipresence of the *Times* is not difficult to explain. It
makes mistakes, but has a passion for the facts. When in the turbulent period after the death of President Kennedy a story in the *Times*
identified Lee Harvey Oswald as "the assassin," Managing Editor
Turner Catledge wrote a reproving letter, printed on the editorial
page, pointing out that Oswald should have been termed "the accused." This even-handed attitude was emphasized again after the
sixteen-week New York newspaper strike of 1962-63. A. H. Raskin's
long report in the *Times* carried this passage about Amory Bradford,
the *Times* Company's Vice President and Raskin's superior: "Mr.
Bradford is handsome, articulate and aloof. . . . One top-level mediator said Mr. Bradford brought such a posture of icy disdain into

the conference rooms that the mediator often felt he ought to ask the hotel to send up more heat."

The *Times* is made even more important because of its consistent sense of responsibility to history, which is demonstrated in every issue and emphasized periodically when the editors rip out pages of advertising to make room for printing significant documents. One ran 247,000 words. That record was broken when the Warren Commission reported, in a huge volume, on the assassination of President Kennedy. Other newspapers were content to publish a supplement made up of excerpts reported by the wire services. The *Times* ignored the cut-down versions and printed the full text.

The special pride that springs from working for the world's greatest newspaper is not apparent to a casual observer. The vast newsroom in New York looks misleadingly like metropolitan newsrooms everywhere: a picture of clutter and concentration. Reporters and editors, many with their shirt sleeves at half-mast, might be producing something dispensable—the *Journal-American* or the *World-Telegram & Sun*. During slack periods, copy editors sometimes amuse themselves by telling history's most important stories in typically brief *Times* headlines:

JEHOVAH RESTING   METHUSELAH DIES: MOSES ON SINAI,
AFTER 6-DAY TASK   JUDEAN WAS 969   GETS 10-PT. PLAN

The difference between the *Times* and other papers begins to become apparent during the late-afternoon news conference. It was long presided over by Catledge and retains his spirit even though, when he was promoted to executive editor in 1964, he gave over the reins of the conference to his successor as managing editor, Clifton Daniel. A big, seemingly pleasant, decisive man whose voice betrays his Mississippi background, Catledge said relatively little but dominated each meeting. He would call on the other editors for summaries of the day's leading events and introduce cautionary notes: "Let's use that word 'torpedo' very carefully." If there were to be light edges, Catledge would initiate them. Under Daniel, the conferences seem to be less formal, but there is the same aura of signifi-

cance, as though each editor is aware that historians in some far
future will be searching the next issue.

The great difference becomes clear when one examines the significant revelations that have dotted the history of the *Times*. President Kennedy was the beneficiary of one. Eleven days before the
invasion of Cuba that his CIA had been shepherding so carefully,
the editors of the *Times* informed him that their correspondents had
discovered that explosive secret and a detailed report was imminent.
Kennedy persuaded them to postpone publication until after the
landing in the Bay of Pigs, but during the succeeding discussions
with *Times* editors and reporters *he* picked up new information about
the mounting of the invasion.

What this chiefly shows is that every official, even the most
powerful, needs a New York *Times*, for he is to some extent insulated
from the realities his own administration creates by the fears and
the ambitions of his subordinates, not to mention the confusion in
communications.

This case also shows the immense power of the *Times*, which,
at its ultimate, enables it to make government decisions. Had the
editors decided to publish everything they knew immediately upon
learning of it, they would, in effect, have vetoed the invasion itself;
no assault landing that has been announced in the press can take
place. In point of fact, the *Times* had earlier signaled invasion preparations. A story that had been published two months before the
landing in the Bay of Pigs was headlined

U.S. HELPS TRAIN AN ANTI-CASTRO FORCE
AT SECRET GUATEMALAN AIRGROUND BASE

Catledge said after the invasion failed that he regretted not
publishing everything. "Our primary obligation," he said, "is to our
readers. I wouldn't know how to interpret our obligation to the
government."

Nothing better illustrates how *Times* decisions affect government
decisions than the famous case of Project Argus.

The project began in the inventive mind of Nicholas Christofilos, a University of California physicist. Self-taught, and long known as "that crazy Greek," Christofilos told fellow scientists that an atomic burst in the near-vacuum of outer space might yield important military knowledge. The effect that most interested Christofilos was the temporary trapping of high-energy electrons at high altitudes in the magnetic field of the earth. An atomic burst would throw off nuclei—some of them radioactive. Decaying with the release of energetic electrons and gamma rays, they would form a veil around the earth and circulate in complicated paths.

Other explorations seemed to validate the idea, but testing Christofilos' theory was touchy. If the world learned that the United States was exploding atomic bombs in the atmosphere, fear of fallout might become world-wide panic. Actually, there was no fall-out hazard, but when the President's Science Advisory Committee decided to undertake the experiment, secrecy was considered essential. And so a Navy task force was created behind a curtain like the one that had concealed the Manhattan Project of World War II. When Project Argus was completed, U.S. officials congratulated themselves on carrying out a mammoth experiment behind a wall of secrecy.

Ironically, several Washington correspondents had been developing clues about the project months before it began. Henry Simmons, a member of the Washington Bureau of *Newsweek*, was exploring it in a copy of the Congressional hearings on appropriations for the Department of Defense. Knowing of the new Advanced Research Projects Agency (ARPA), but not its mission, he read every word of the hearings relating to it. There wasn't much; the agency works in classified fields, and its appropriations are reported in brief. But he found a two-inch chart breaking down the agency's $520 million budget. Item Three was "Military developments for and applications of space technology, $138.2 million." The fourth subheading carried the cryptic title "Project Argus."

"I had never heard the name before, so naturally I fixed on it right away," Simmons says. "We tried to figure it every possible way, trying to figure whether A-R-G-U-S was a set of initials, like M-I-D-A-S. Finally, we went to the dictionary and found: 'Argus, many-eyed creature of mythology.' "

During an eight-month period, Simmons mailed nine reports on experiments similar to Argus to *Newsweek*'s science editor, occasionally touching on the mystery project. These were private papers—not for publication. In one, he reported after the Argus experiments had caused radio disturbances: "There is a lot more to these shoots than either the Air Force or ARPA is giving out . . . it is obvious that the radiation experiments are only one aspect of the picture. . . . There is ARPA's Project Argus, for example."

But Simmons knew only that Project Argus existed; he could not develop the full framework. Knowing that others, including reporters for the highly respected *Aviation Week*, were also tracing clues, Simmons asked only guarded questions during press conferences: "I got pretty close once, but then I looked around at the others at that conference and saw Walter Sullivan of the *Times*. I stopped then. I was afraid he might guess the story from what I was asking."

Actually, Sullivan was even edgier than Simmons about Simmons's questions. Sullivan and Hanson Baldwin, military editor of the *Times*, had been sitting on the Argus story for weeks. What they did with it illustrates several things, including the value of the specialist.

It was Hanson Baldwin's story. A 1924 graduate of Annapolis, the lean, tough Baldwin has had a pipeline to the highest reaches of the military since he became the *Times*'s military analyst in 1937. His paper's prestige accounts for some of his standing, but none of his rivals who cover the Pentagon delude themselves that this is his only advantage. As one says, "He knows just as much about theory and tactics as the admirals and generals he talks to; maybe more." Baldwin travels abroad on stories and shuttles back and forth between New York and Washington. On one of his visits to Washington he learned of Project Argus from his Navy friends. No scientific specialist, Baldwin went to Turner Catledge and asked for help. Catledge assigned Sullivan as legman and scientific consultant.

The Argus experiment was still several weeks in the future when Sullivan interviewed a friend who was then a key figure in the space program. "He was both horrified and amused that we knew of Project Argus," Sullivan says. "Firing atomic bombs above the atmosphere and so far from our shores raised grave diplomatic problems. He said that, in his opinion, publication of the plan in advance might force cancellation of the experiment." The story was not published then, and the experiment went off on schedule. But publishing the facts might still cause an international furor. Sullivan and Baldwin held off.

Later, Sullivan attended a press conference at the annual meeting of the American Association for the Advancement of Science. Henry Simmons was there, asking questions that made it seem that *Newsweek* was alarmingly close to publishing a story on Argus.

At this point, the *Times*, which had been solicitous about the government reaction, had to weigh also its desire to beat the opposition. Sullivan wrote a letter to a high official in the Department of Defense—and delivered it by hand—warning that the *Times* had reached the point "where we no longer believe we can continue to withhold at least a partial treatment of Argus." Then he met with U.S. officials, who argued strongly against publication.

Not satisfied, Sullivan asked several leading scientists, nearly all of whom agreed that the only reason for withholding the story was to avoid embarrassment to the government. Then he attended a lecture by Dr. James R. Killian, Jr., the President's science advisor. Appearing on the dais at the end of the lecture, Sullivan handed Killian a letter reading in part: "We doubt that we can continue to withhold at least a limited account of Argus."

Soon, Baldwin and Sullivan agreed that they should recommend publication. The ultimate decision was made in their meeting with the publisher and the managing editor. Sullivan relates, "It was agreed that, as a courtesy to the government, I should notify Dr. Killian of our intent."

Thus, with a story that began: "Secret nuclear test detonations at more than 300 miles above the earth were conducted by the United States early last September," the New York *Times* decided what was to be the day of diplomatic reckoning for the U.S. government.

Like every other *Times*man, Reston takes strength from his paper. But more than any other, he strengthens the *Times*. It is not only his mastery of news-gathering techniques but the way he writes the news he gathers that influences the press corps. As a Kennedy assistant once said, "Reston writes a column about Kennedy losing the liberals in the Democratic Party. A week later you see two others writing the same story, and ten days later, six correspondents are saying the same thing."

The point is illustrated by Reston's column, which appeared in the summer of 1963, on Nelson Rockefeller's quest of the Republican Presidential nomination:

> Nelson Rockefeller was in Washington this week, but his old friends scarcely recognized him. He talked like Harold Stassen and acted like Dick Nixon.
>
> The Presidential bug has really got him. You could tell because he denied it. He was in town to gather support for his campaign. Everybody knew it, and he knew everybody knew it, but he followed the old deceptive ritual even though it was obvious to everybody, including himself, that he was deceiving nobody.
>
> There seems to be something about the Presidential fever that drives men away from their true beliefs toward the beliefs of their detractors. If a man is a liberal, he seems determined to prove he's a conservative, and vice versa.
>
> Harold Stassen started on the left and when he began to get the White House itch, he lurched over to the right. Nixon started on the right, and then turned left in trying to beat Kennedy, and right again in trying to beat Pat Brown in California, thereby proving that it's easy to lose both ways.

Reston then quoted the New York Governor to show how the new Rockefeller was like the Nixon who used the slippery device of "the attack that was not quite an attack, of the charge that was not really a charge—and did it all with a smile and a 'hope' that it was not all true." The effect was soon apparent. Story after story equating the new Rockefeller with the old Nixon flowed out of Washington bureaus. A *Newsweek* report quoted the most savage paragraph from

Reston's column: "The tolerance for political baloney in Washington is pretty high. The town has produced and swallowed more than its share. Politicians all stoop to conquer sooner or later, but Rockefeller seemed to be stooping pretty low pretty soon."

The multiplier effect of Reston's writing springs in part from his wry bluntness; he can treat all but the heaviest subjects with an offhand grace that deftly summarizes what many others have been half-thinking. Attacking the penchant for labeling ("The tags provided by the National Committee almost always prove to be tidier than the truth"), Reston wrote: "The Capital is now engaged in the usual quadrennial diversion of hanging political labels on the Presidential candidates and dividing them into heroes and villains. This labeling operation is part of the story-telling and myth-making industry in Washington—a vast enterprise—and is a great convenience because it enables the voter to avoid thinking or dealing with the facts."

During the last year of the second Eisenhower Administration, when the President was at his most retiring, Reston conducted inventive analyses of Presidential prospects through a device he called Uniquack. "Who's going to win the election?" he asked the machine. Uniquack decided that the new Chief Executive would be John Kennedy because "Every President in this century has a double letter in his name. William McKinley—two l's in William. Theodore Roosevelt—two o's. Then there were Woodrow Wilson, Warren Harding, Calvin Coolidge, Herbert Hoover, Franklin Roosevelt, and, of course, Harry."

"What about Eisenhower? Wasn't he President?"

Uniquack: "We must await the judgment of history on that."

Reston summed up President Johnson's startling blend of liberalism and conservatism with: "President Johnson today gave his first State of the Union message sort of a Franklin Delano Hoover twist. It was the New Deal revisited with emphasis on the Forgotten Man, and flashes of Roosevelt in a three-inch Hoover collar."

Despite the free flow of his prose, Reston is not a facile writer. Krock says: "He's not the sort of fellow who gets a smattering of a story, looks into his soul, claps his hands, and then writes brilliantly.

He's the industrious type, always working. He'll call thirty people to get a single line in a story. And he's running all the time."

One of Reston's light columns on journalism has the ring of autobiography: "It makes no difference how many hours a man has to write a story or fix a story up for publication. That story, late or soon, momentous or frivolous, will develop a life of its own. It will kill time. It will refuse to go down on paper. It will develop inaccuracies, and it will suggest historical parallels which the writer will not be able to run down in the library. . . . News stories expand and time contracts, meeting inexorably each day precisely twenty minutes after a man is supposed to be home for dinner."

It is clear, too, that Reston is a studied writer, always aware of the effects he produces. He varies those effects by leaving Washington at least once a month because "Being here all the time is like talking to yourself on the telephone." He admits that readers' reactions are much on his mind: "Most columnists haven't learned what every good major-league pitcher knows—that you have to have a change of pace, and you can't use your fast ball all the time. They tend to lead their readership to anticipate them. I think if I took a look at the news week I could tell you what David Lawrence's position would be. Alsop is a Cassandra. He doesn't have to keep a belief in the human race—keep it going—he hasn't any children. I have a moral conviction and a religious conviction which he doesn't have. Around Christmas and Easter I write about what justification there is for growth, change, and renewal."

Some of the correspondents who admire Reston most find his moralistic columns hard going. One referred to his salute to the astronauts as "puerile" and complained that he could get through only the first two sentences of the Christmas column of 1963: "I could see that Scotty was off again on one of his inspirational things." (The column began: "Christmas is no time to tell the truth about the politicians in Washington, so maybe it is the time to tell the truth about their wives. They are the shining figures at the top of this year's Christmas tree.")

Nonetheless, Reston changes his pace so often that those correspondents who skip his column one day are likely to return for the next. "Those wonderful leads!" a correspondent exclaimed. "Reston can summarize *anything* in a sentence." Then he pulled from his stack of clippings the Reston column of May 22, 1962, which began: "The most serious problem in Washington today—because it affects all other problems—is the gap between present political realities and past political assumptions."

If the basis of Reston's influence is apparent in his talent, the basis of the talent is not nearly so clear. Unlike a number of correspondents, he was never a prodigy. In fact, Turner Catledge, the plain-speaking executive editor of the *Times*, says that "Reston is trying to live down his past."

Certainly, Reston's past is almost embarrassingly ordinary, distinguished only by hard work. Born in Scotland to a poverty-ridden, strongly religious family, he spent much of his youth in Ohio. His mother pushed him with: "Don't be a common workman. It's no sin to be poor, but it is one to stay poor." He did everything from delivering papers to caddying at the local golf course, but his industry seemed to be leading nowhere beyond the eighteenth hole. He became a good golfer (once even considered making golf his business)—and a poor scholar. At the University of Illinois, his only A in his major, journalism, was in sports writing. Reston by-passed the course in governmental reporting and took not a single course in political science. His graduation in 1932 was distinctively without honors.

Writing about games fascinated him for a time. He was a sports writer for the Springfield (Ohio) *Daily News*, and he worked in sports publicity for the Cincinnati Reds and for Ohio State University. Then Wilson Hicks, director of the Associated Press Feature Service, hired him to work in New York, covering sports, general news, and writing a weekly Broadway column.

The great change began in 1935 when Reston married an Illinois classmate, Sally Fulton, a pretty, intelligent girl who had been president of her sorority and had made Phi Beta Kappa with ease. Reston, who had never been confused with the man most likely to succeed, increased his ambitions. "For years," one friend has commented, "Scotty was trying to live up to Sally."

Twice during his days in New York with AP, Reston tried to land a job on the *Times*. Both applications were rejected. Then, in 1937, the AP sent him to London with an unusual two-part assignment: writing sports and filling in the slack periods by covering the British Foreign Office. His ambition was clear. One former AP man declares: "Why, ten days after Reston got to London as a sports writer, he was sending back pieces on the international situation by mail." By 1939 the *Times* deemed him ready and he joined the London Bureau.

Reston was far from an instant success. The *Times* sent him to Washington in 1941, but after a short stay only chance prevented his reassignment to the less prestigious Boston Bureau. Ironically, his rise on the *Times* actually began when he left the paper temporarily to work for the U.S. government in reorganizing the London Bureau of the Office of War Information. U.S. Ambassador John Winant described him to *Times* Publisher Arthur Hays Sulzberger as "intent, handsome, square thinking, adept, and well liked." Not long after that, Reston was brought back from London to work as the publisher's assistant.

Working as Sulzberger's "s.o.b. administrative man," as the publisher himself described the position, was a dizzying height in the *Times'* hierarchy, but it was not high enough for Reston. He read endlessly to prepare himself for top-level reporting. A former *Times* man who was making extensive use of the paper's library in 1943 has said: "Suddenly, every volume on the Versailles Peace Conference was being taken out by some new guy on the paper—Reston. Maybe a day or two later the books would be back, but all marked up, and every time his pencil hit just the juicy passage, the good quote, the big turning point." Not long after, Reston wangled his way back to London as acting head of the *Times* Bureau. He performed so well that he was sent to Washington in 1944 as Diplomatic Correspondent, just in time for the Dumbarton Oaks Conference.

During nine years of covering the diplomatic beat in Washington, Reston won every major honor in journalism. He turned down high-paying positions—from Washington Bureau Chief of *Time* Magazine to syndicated columnist—but his ambition was not really satisfied. Arthur Krock, who had been running the Washington

Bureau for more than twenty years, was well over sixty, but he seemed likely to go on forever. Reston made his own ambition clear one day by saying lightly to Krock, "You look too damned healthy." Then, in 1953, the publisher of the Washington *Post* asked Reston to become its editor. Krock called a staff meeting and announced: "Mr. Reston has received several very attractive offers to work elsewhere, one of them particularly tempting. I did not want the *Times* to lose his immensely valuable services, and I knew that I was in a position to offer him strong inducement to stay with the *Times* for life. On my own motion, Mr. James Reston will become The Washington Correspondent of the New York *Times* with complete charge."

Reston made profound changes. One is emphasized every time his column appears on the editorial page beside a column by Krock, who has continued commenting on events:

WASHINGTON By James Reston	IN THE NATION By Arthur Krock
President Johnson is not likely to leave the Vietnam problem where it is. The last *coup d'etat* in November was a tragedy. The second one this week was almost a joke—sort of a cabinet shuffle with tanks—and the United States is beginning to look not only inefficient but slightly foolish.	The heavy emphasis on domestic problems and remedial programs in President Johnson's first State of the Union message (Jan. 8) induced the general assumption that he expected no new, immediate international crises which would divert his concentration on pushing these programs through Congress. If this assumption was sound, its basis has now been shattered by explosive events all around the world.
President Kennedy, who was a patient and vaguely pessimistic man, might have gone on supporting a nation that would not defend itself, but President Johnson, who is neither patient nor pessimistic, is not likely to go on paying out over $1,000,000 a day to perpetuate a stalemate.	The East-West disarmament negotiations just resumed at Geneva have been brutally interrupted by the latest Soviet mockery of their concept— the gunfire which destroyed a strayed, unarmed United States training plane and killed its crew. And this incident presages a continuation of the sterile record of these consultations, broken only by a nuclear test-ban treaty which already appears to ban the use of atomic power even for the peaceful purposes of excavating a new, lower-cost Isthmian canal. . . .
Accordingly, we are probably coming to the end of the period when the United States would neither fight nor negotiate. And we are probably approaching a new phase where both fighting and negotiating will be stepped up. . . .	

Reston, the incisive observer whose clarity and sure grasp of language inform weighty subjects; Krock, the ponderous commentator whose significance is sometimes heavy-handed and fuzzy—this is one mark of change. Another is the "Observer" column written by Russell Baker of the Washington Bureau, which appears three times a week on the editorial page, light-edged and pointed, as in this primer on politics:

Run, Alice, run. Run and see the Senate. See Senator Goldwater. Do you see Senator Goldwater running? No. Senator Goldwater is talking. Do not be deceived. He is running very hard toward the White House.

Jump, Spot, jump. Jump for the gentlemen of the Democratic National Committee. See how miserable they look. They are unhappy because they do not have enough Democrats at the Capitol to save the program. They have only two Democrats for each Republican. Will the program be saved if more Democrats come to the Capitol next year? No one can tell. Democrats are strange creatures. Often they are Republicans wearing Democratic false faces. Is Washington not a wonderful place?

During Reston's tenure as Bureau Chief—he was made associate editor in 1964—news-story style in Washington stories also became several shades lighter:

Harold E. Stassen pumped his sagging Herter-for-Vice-President balloon full of statistics and sent it aloft again today. It was promptly shot down. . . .

Out of the State Department last week there came a secret, a phone call, a book and a murmur of complaint—little symptoms of a big problem: the unordered process by which U.S. foreign policy is determined.

From now on, the words "meanwhile, back at the ranch" are likely to pop up frequently in stories about America's first family.

The semantic change springs in part from a *Times*-wide emphasis on bright passages, largely from the fact that Reston shaped the Washington staff. When he became Bureau Chief at the age of forty-three, Reston was one of the younger *Times* reporters in Washington. Now, at fifty-five, he is one of the oldest. Retirement has removed a few of the veterans, and death has taken others. William S. White quit to write a syndicated column. William H. Lawrence became a television newscaster. But Reston took a hand in some of the departures. "He was strong-minded about building his own bureau," one correspondent says. "Men with decades in this town were reassigned to New York or sent abroad. A few left on their own because Reston was making it clear that the future was with the bright young men he was bringing in."

Some of the young men are brilliant. Reston considers his bureau "the finest staff of young reporters in America." That may be a modest assessment. A rival says: "The young specialists he has brought into his bureau make it the best newsgathering agency in the world."

Reston's care in building the bureau is illustrated by his search for a science writer. "I went to every major atomic physicist and asked whether I should hire a physicist and teach him to write or hire a reporter and let him learn science. They agreed that it would be better to get a reporter." And so Reston took on John Finney of United Press International, who, one rival science writer complains, "is so far ahead of the rest of us that we'll never catch up."

In 1954, Reston hired Anthony Lewis of the Washington *Daily News*, who was then in the process of winning a Pulitzer Prize; the announcement of the award came even as Lewis was visiting the *Times* Bureau to clear up the details of his new job. He was allowed to go off to Harvard for a year on a Nieman Fellowship to study law. After returning he won another Pulitzer Prize. Justice Felix Frankfurter once said of his Supreme Court reporting: "There are not two members of the Court itself who could get the gist of each decision so accurately in so few words."

Reston's insight into the talents of young reporters is shown by the career of David Halberstam. A tall, husky, excitable New Yorker,

Halberstam was graduated from Harvard in 1955 and headed straight for Mississippi on the theory that the Southern civil-rights story was the greatest of the time. He worked for several months on a small Mississippi paper, then moved to the Nashville *Tennesseean.* Throughout a five-year period he wrote articles on the race crisis for *The Reporter.* Reston, who reads prodigiously in searching for young talent—"One brilliant writer," he says, "is worth four competent guys"—saw *The Reporter* pieces and one day called the *Tennesseean* office and asked to speak to Halberstam. "This is Scotty Reston," he said. Halberstam retorted, "I got no Goddamned time for jokes," and slammed down the receiver. Reston patiently called back, and a short time later Halberstam joined the *Times* Washington Bureau.

Halberstam was not an instant success. Reston suggested, "Dave, maybe you need a hotter climate and darker people." Halberstam asked to go to the Congo. There, he wrote eyewitness accounts of the Katanga fighting, suffered a minor wound when a jet strafed the Elizabethville airport, and won a Page One Award for best foreign reporting.

Then he was transferred to Saigon and probed so relentlessly into official intrigue there and covered the fighting so well that the struggle for Vietnam became known for a time as "Halberstam's War." Many of his reports contradicted the optimistic reports of U.S. officials, who were counting heavily on the established government to roll back the Communist assaults. One Presidential aide held: "That man is trying to bring down the Diem government all by himself." When Diem was overthrown late in 1963, his sister-in-law, Madame Nhu, blazed, "Halberstam should be barbecued, and I would be glad to supply the fluid and the match." Later when it became clear that Halberstam had been right all along—neither U.S. nor Vietnamese spokesmen had been entirely candid about Vietnam's internal troubles or the progress of the war with the Communists— he won a Pulitzer Prize.

Endless influence is dangerous in any hands. However noble the intentions of a journalist or a journalistic institution, the amassing of great power carries its own danger. Fortunately, though, the structure of influence in political journalism is tenuous. Should Reston or the *Times* demonstrate a concern for power for its own sake, by so much would their influence be reduced. Reston guards against the possibility by working according to reasoned *Weltanschauung* about the role of the reporter: "He does not owe [his] primary allegiance to the owner of his newspaper, or to his managing editor, or to his government, or to the sources of his information; he owes it to the people." Reston's paper has been demonstrating the same kind of concern since 1851. In a materialist society, perhaps the best proof of that concern is in the balance sheet: Some years, the net earnings of the New York *Times*—an institution with more than eight hundred reporters and editors—are less than David Brinkley's.

CHAPTER FIVE

David Brinkley and Friends

"One of the great things about a newspaper . . . is that you can split the thing up and let everybody in the family settle into a quiet trance with the section he likes best. The television makes us all feel a little obsolescent once in a while, but it stuns the mind. It makes you listen to all the news you don't want to hear in order to get around to the news you do want to hear. You can't split up Chet Huntley or throw away part of Dave Brinkley."

—JAMES RESTON

"Every medium has to live with its weaknesses and exploit its strengths. Television's strengths are, of course, its immediacy and its ability to deliver both picture and sound to a very wide audience. Its weakness is that it cannot deliver anything like the volume of news found in good metropolitan newspapers, that it cannot be laid aside and perused at a more convenient time. . . .

"But that is what we are, an orange, and it would be pleasing if our critics would stop complaining because we are not an apple."

—WILLIAM MC ANDREW of NBC

"When a session goes on hour after hour Mr. Brinkley somehow retains his crispness and manages to avoid succumbing to the creeping weariness that humanly enough overtakes his counterparts. Perhaps personality should not be a factor in TV journalism, but in a medium-rooted communication between one person in the studio and another in the home it is futile to dispute the importance of the basic human equation. Mr. Brinkley wears the best because he seems the most alive."

—TV Critic JACK GOULD

To the massive audience that keeps vaguely up to date by watching the six-o'clock report, a network newsman is an enviable figure. But one commentator holds that, even though television journalists became a public treasure from the moment they covered a political convention and the elite of the broadcasting business when everything else became suspect after the quiz-show scandals, "God knows when we'll be accepted by the Washington press corps."

This is almost out of date, but it still has a certain acid accuracy. Some reporters treat TV news as a vaguely shady operation, superficial show business masquerading as journalism between the halitosis commercials. And most of the television newsmen who began their reporting careers working for newspapers, wire services, or magazines are a bit embarrassed by their new wealth and glamour, like the only man at the office party who showed up in a tuxedo.

Envy of the glamour of television is partly to blame for the antagonism of some newspapermen. Not even the columnist with the widest circulation can hope for the attention, or the instant recognition, that envelops most TV personalities. "When they're on the road in a political campaign," Columnist Robert Novak says, "they sign more autographs than the candidates."

More important in assessing antagonism is the fact that television has altered the basic structure of political journalism. Reston points out: "The whole walkie-talkie thing affects events—whenever anything happens, there is a rush by television reporters, and by their presence they add to the drama." This became violently clear during the 1964 Republican Convention in San Francisco, where television personnel outnumbered the delegates, 1,825 to 1,308. Some of the delegates responded to General Eisenhower's attack on "sensation-seeking columnists and commentators" with the most savage show of fist-shaking belligerence American reporters have ever faced. For a time, the presence of the mass media was the convention's most notable feature. One delegate called Novak the name that, for peaceful relations, must be accompanied by a smile. He didn't smile, and Novak hit him. No political party can afford, however, to show such overt antagonism to reporters for long. After John Chancellor of NBC was hustled off the convention floor (quipping as he went, "This is John Chancellor, somewhere in custody"), the chief sergeant-at-arms sped to his side and personally escorted him back.

How TV alters politics itself became apparent the following month at the Democratic Convention in Atlantic City. The entire proceedings were tailored to the demands of television, not just in planning the program and equipping the hall but in managing events as well. As Reston commented: "I don't think, in pre-television days, there would have been any hesitation in seeing that the Mississippi Freedom Party delegation was removed from the floor. To go through the business of physically removing the delegation in front of the cameras was more than the Democratic Party was willing to face."

This should not be surprising. The value of a façade has long been significant. As Machiavelli wrote: "Everyone sees what you seem to be . . . the mass of mankind is always swayed by appearances." Thus it was that Abraham Lincoln credited one event and one man with making him President. The event was the famous Cooper Union speech. The man was the greatest of the early American photographers, Mathew Brady. Lincoln had long been derided as ugly and ungainly, but Brady took a picture that showed him as a man of dignity and strong presence.

The power of pictures has been magnified many times by the nation-wide saturation of television—Americans own more television sets than bathtubs—affecting political life profoundly. The smallest nuance has become vital. General Dwight Eisenhower wore rimless eyeglasses for years, and looked old-fashioned. His television consultant, Robert Montgomery, bought him a pair of horn-rims. Supporters of John Kennedy made much of the thick pancake make-up worn by Richard Nixon during the Great Debates of 1960. They failed to mention that Kennedy was so concerned with lighting effects that he made special trips to the studios ahead of time; there he and his brother Robert took turns in observing each other at the lectern from control-booth monitors. Senator Barry Goldwater asked, just before he was scheduled to accept the Presidential nomination at the Republican Convention in 1964, that television cameramen not photograph him from a low angle and not switch to reaction scenes of the audience during the speech. (The networks denied both requests, which may have enhanced Goldwater's already strong distaste for TV.) President Johnson has told cameramen that his best side is his left and that he prefers to be photographed at angles of no less than forty-five degrees. One important item in campaign budgets these days is a large fee for an expert lighting consultant.

If all this seems vaguely silly, the real importance of appearance today should make it less so. Since television became widespread during the 1950's, the gallery of Presidential nominees has become strikingly photogenic. Of the last four—Kennedy, Nixon, Johnson, and Goldwater—only Kennedy can be considered stunningly handsome, but all are at least a cut above the average American in appearance. More important, they are several cuts above most of the candidates of earlier times. In the Age of Television, it is impossible to imagine either party nominating obese William Howard Taft or sour Calvin Coolidge or bulb-nosed Al Smith. There is much more to winning a nomination for high political office than pleasing looks, of course, or Hollywood might furnish most of the candidates. It is nonetheless instructive to review a gallery of portraits of today's United States Senate. There is cause to wonder whether Hollywood's environs boast handsomer men than George Smathers, Thruston Morton, Joseph Clark, Harrison Williams, Robert Kennedy, Eugene McCarthy, Stuart Symington, Frank Church, Mike Monroney, Gale McGee, and Henry Jackson; or mature men of distinction more distinguished-looking than J. W. Fulbright, Paul Douglas, and Spessard Holland. Pierre Salinger probably persuaded all the other bulging cigar-smokers who hope to win political office not to appear on television with trim, clean-cut looking opponents like George Murphy. One of Murphy's aides admitted after their debates in the race for Senator from California in 1964 that Murphy had not been nearly so interested in *debating* as in standing side-by-side with Salinger before a TV camera. And surely there is a political lesson in the fact that a well-entrenched but painfully plain conservative like Homer Capehart from a basically conservative state like Indiana lost to handsome, liberal Birch Bayh in 1962. Leaving television out of an equation that attempts to explain this change seems senseless. When the patriarchs like Harry Byrd, Richard Russell, and Everett Dirksen at last go down, it will probably be by the cut of a profile.

Exactly when television began to assert its great power is difficult to determine. Was it during the late Senator Estes Kefauver's crime investigation hearings? During the Army-McCarthy hearings? Certainly, television helped make Kefauver a national figure and helped destroy Senator Joe McCarthy. One suspects, though, that the full dimensions of television in elective politics were being formed in 1952. It was then that Senator Henry Cabot Lodge of Massachusetts, up for re-election, agreed to debate his Democratic opponent, a callow young Congressman named John F. Kennedy. Political experts called the Lodge-Kennedy debates a draw. But for a thirty-five-year-old Congressman to stand on the same platform with a fifty-year-old Senator and do as well is, in effect, a victory for the Congressman. Kennedy won the election and entered the Senate.

It was also in 1952 that Vice Presidential Candidate Richard Nixon began to turn television to his advantage. Caught in a controversy over the notorious "Nixon Fund," he went on television to attempt to show that he measured up to General Eisenhower's prescription for the Republican Party: that everyone be "clean as a hound's tooth." Perhaps the most curious aspect of this entire episode was that Eisenhower would not himself judge Nixon's cleanliness; he wanted a running mate who could make himself *appear* to be clean before a national television audience. And Nixon, with an emotional address that has come to be known as "The Checkers Speech," did win his audience. Whereupon Eisenhower embraced him.

The great impact of television became more obvious in 1960. Unable to find a graceful way to avoid debating Kennedy after Congress had set aside the "equal time" provision of the Communications Act, Nixon was clearly defeated in the most decisive of the Great Debates, the first—and before an audience of seventy to seventy-five million. He licked his lips, perspired, looked ghostly because of the too-heavy application of make-up, and, in trying to destroy his image as a politician who goes for the jugular, said "me, too" once too often. Kennedy, much less well known, and with nothing to lose, was so articulate, confident, and coolly aggressive that in a single hour he managed to shake off the image of an immature man who might not be able to stand up to other world leaders, especially Khrushchev. Before the debates, the Gallup Poll was showing Nixon leading Kennedy by 47 per cent to 46 per cent. The week after the first debate, Gallup showed Kennedy ahead of Nixon, 49 per cent to 46 per cent. Elmo Roper found that nearly four million voters decided how to cast their ballots on the basis of the debates, and three million of them voted for Kennedy.

A politician adds to the store of bile that has been accumulating in many newspaper and magazine correspondents every time he brushes by them to preen for the television cameras. And he is quite likely to brush by them. James Wechsler of the New York *Post* says, "It's a general judgment among politicians that to get on television for three minutes is better than getting seven inches of type in a newspaper."

Newspaper and magazine correspondents grump almost unanimously that it seems to be only a matter of time until the entire political world will be rigged for a television show. They contend that public affairs are no longer natural events at all, but performances. Although this ignores the fact that few political events have ever been pure and spontaneous—a politician is apt to put on a personality for a pen-and-notebook interview as well as for a camera —television clearly multiplies falsity.

What happens to politicians when they move in camera range was shown during one of President Johnson's formal messages to Congress. He asked for "unswerving support of the United Nations" and for "strong, forward-looking actions on the foreign-aid bill, making it clear that we are not forfeiting our responsibilities to this hemisphere or to the world. . . ." On that occasion, Congress was shown on television, and members of the House of Representatives applauded as vigorously as did the Senate. Three weeks later, with no camera eye to pick them out, Congressmen applauded Representative Otto Passman of Louisiana, who had just led the way in slashing heavily into U.S. support for agencies of the United Nations and in cutting the foreign-aid bill by half. No wonder the correspondents laugh when politicians fail on television, as they did when Senator Everett Dirksen and Congressman Charles Halleck were so inept in their regular television reports on Republican action in Congress that one reporter described them as "that old ruin of a Shakespearean actor and W. C. Fields."

The disdain in the press corps for television news is complex, and not altogether free of hypocrisy. Some correspondents for the print media (who consider "print media" yet another sign of electronic journalism) angle for opportunities to appear on "Meet the Press" even as they complain that they are becoming second-class citizens. And when Martha Rountree, one of the creators of "Meet the Press," went on the air with an abortive program called "Press Conference," she had no trouble lining up correspondents to act the part for the cameras. Even the most serene of the correspondents has been affected. Walter Lippmann was so hesitant about being interviewed on a special CBS program that network officials, who hoped to lure him into appearing annually for a one-hour interview, feared that he would not even go through with the first. But he did appear, and the program was a sparkling success. Several months later, he asked with some eagerness when the time would be right for another interview.

In 1964, the newspaper world, which had long professed disdain for television news, was forced to swallow a bitter lump of pride. For almost a decade, the networks had been increasing the speed of election reporting. Television viewers who went to bed during the early morning hours every election night with memories of the huge ballot totals that had appeared on their screens awakened to find that their newspapers were reporting fewer votes hours later. Something like a war took place during the early 1960's. When newspaper editorial writers were not confusing two quite distinct network operations— one reporting actual vote totals, another projecting eventual vote totals from a small sample—they were charging the networks with falsifying returns. Nobody, they contended, could count votes that fast. Actually, by limiting their counting to the major contests— usually those for President, Governor, Senator, and Congressman— and by spending enormous sums, the networks were counting votes more rapidly than anyone had ever counted them. Instead of sending reporters to the official tabulating centers where election officials amass and count votes brought in from precincts—the time-honored method—the networks were sending thousands of reporters to the precincts. The precinct reporters telephoned the results to huge network tabulating centers, where they were counted and flashed on television screens long before most of the precinct totals reached the official tabulating center.

The difference between the television reports and the newspaper reports could not be allowed to continue; newspapers could not afford to lag so far behind. Publishers put increasing pressure on the wire services—AP and UPI—to speed the vote-counting. But the network method was costly; NBC spent nearly $500,000 to report the 1964 California Presidential primary alone, and CBS spent more. The newspapers were not willing—and some of them were unable—to pay the assessments that would enable the wire services to compete with the networks. And so during the summer of 1964, after NBC, CBS, and ABC had combined forces to reduce the enormous costs to each of reporting the 1964 general election in November, AP asked to join the combine. UPI followed with the same request. The networks allowed both to join, but gave neither a vote on the executive board that was to decide how the election would be covered. The board assigned the two wire services to cover the balloting in twenty-three small states and in the District of Columbia; the three networks took nine states each.

Since virtually all U.S. daily newspapers are served by either AP or UPI, or both, this meant that the combine, dominated by the networks, supplied the nation's newspapers with election returns. Sensitive to the ancient disdain of the "real newsmen" for television, network officials added salt, decreeing that the election reports must be attributed to "Network Election Service," and letting it be known that the new partners in the enterprise had to be taught how to cover an election the modern way. "We practically had to set up schools to teach them how to report precinct-by-precinct," one network official said.

The continuing rift between the printed and the electronic media dates back to the beginning of radio news in the 1920's. Then, as now, the attitudes of the newspaper world were complex. Some newspapermen held that radio amounted to little, and that the little would become less once the novelty wore off. After a six-month trial, the Richmond *Times-Dispatch* relinquished its "telephone license" (one of three granted to operate radio stations in the South) on the ground that there was no discernible future for radio. Other newspapers had a grimmer thought that was no more accurate; they feared that the spread of broadcasting would cause the death of daily newspapers.

Most of the Washington correspondents of that time seemed to adhere to the *Times-Dispatch* philosophy. They laughingly dismissed proposals that radio reporters be allowed to join the National Press Club and to cover Congressional sessions from the press galleries. Radio was an ephemeral toy. Some correspondents took part-time jobs as newscasters when the pay was high enough, but the casualness of their attitudes was probably expressed by the correspondent who reacted to a charge that his newscast was inaccurate with, "What does it matter on radio?"

Public officials dismissed radio almost as emphatically. It was considered a screwball business, and with some justification during the early years. The emphasis was not on content but on whether a program could be heard at all. When President Warren Harding broadcast a political speech from St. Louis in 1923, Senator William Calder of New York wired, "We heard you as plainly as if you had been in our living room"—ignoring what Harding said. When Senator Clarence Dill made the first broadcast from a train, he received a congratulatory telegram that read, "Congratulations on your moving address."

The networks gradually built sizable staffs in Washington, but they received little attention for years, even from those in quest of publicity. A Congressman could see a newspaper clipping; when he talked into a microphone, he was not always sure how his speeches came out—or whether anyone was listening. So many public officials forgot or ignored appointments to make radio addresses and to take part in forums on public affairs that the networks began sending limousines to transport them to the studios. Not until 1939 did Congress get around to voting gallery facilities for the radio correspondents.

Newspaper correspondents shunned the new medium even longer. In fact, it was their resistance to the idea of opening up the press galleries to the interlopers that led to the establishment of separate galleries. And not until 1948 were the radio correspondents brought into the National Press Club.

Some of the offended hold that this resistance sprang from fear of the growing power of radio. The answer is probably simpler: Only the network men who were pick-and-shovel reporters were respected. Too many of the star commentators were simply announcers—pleasant to hear, but unknowing about the business of gathering news. The competence of radio news broadcasting of twenty years ago is not indicated by the few fine reporters on the CBS staff— many of them in Europe—but by the scant attention radio gave the atomic bombing of Hiroshima. One commentator devoted one minute of air time to the bomb and ten minutes to the death of Senator Hiram Johnson of California.

Remembering how Lowell Thomas, Boake Carter, Gabriel Heatter, and other rounded voices of authority had kept much of America close by the radio during the 1930's, too many executives in the dawning era of television journalism reasoned that, since TV was visual radio, a commentator must be a mellow voice, a pleasant profile, and a pose.

Unfortunately, the small screen has the same effect on most commentators that it has on most politicians, revealing instantly to knowledgeable viewers whether the speaker knows what he is talking about or is simply reading words. News and mouthwash commercials were at first intoned with the same authority. And when the "news announcers" tried to lend authenticity by covering live events along with veteran reporters, they proved to be fascinatingly incompetent. "What about Harriman?" one asked Presidential Candidate Adlai Stevenson during a 1956 press conference. Puzzled, Stevenson responded, "Well, what about him?"

Predictably, the proud Washington press corps carried on a nagging warfare with the newcomers. They hooted in print at the apologetic journalism of TV, which may have been epitomized by the CBS commentator who began questioning the Chairman of the Republican National Committee with: "I don't want to throw you a curve, but . . ." Of which Columnist Jim Bishop wrote in his haughtiest Old Newspaper Pro style: "He should. That's his job."

During the 1950's, newspaper, wire-service, and magazine reporters delighted in frustrating TV sound technicians with small whistles, toy metal crickets, and press-conference questions that were

larded with profanity. Some even put still photographers up to flash-
ing their stroboscopic lights into live cameras, and tripped over cables
adroitly enough to pull plugs from wall sockets. Their defense for
these tactics was simple: They were trying to keep television from
turning Washington journalism into a tributary of Madison Avenue.

James Hagerty was President Eisenhower's press secretary during much of this unhappy period and kept his opinions to himself. But
he was quietly disgusted with the "pretty-announcer" era of television
news and, taking over the news department of the American Broadcasting Company at the end of the Eisenhower Presidency, he said
so. ABC would have none of the pseudo-newsmen with the pear-
shaped tones and the regular profiles, Hagerty promised, but would
hire real reporters to go out and get the story and put it on the air.
The new look would win faithful audiences, Hagerty was sure, because the public senses the authority of the prober who has been
to the source.

Among others, Hagerty took on for ABC John Scali of the Associated Press and William H. Lawrence of the New York *Times*, both
famous for getting the news fast and first-hand, both with Bela
Lugosi's chance in a Mr. America contest.

Most television viewers did react emphatically to the opportunity to watch plain, hard-digging reporters reveal their scoops on
ABC-TV; they switched to NBC and CBS.

Only a few months after starting his revolution in TV news,
Hagerty went on the air over a closed circuit and warned stations
affiliated with ABC to broadcast the news programs he had fashioned
or he would quit. It didn't quite come to that. Hagerty was finally
kicked upstairs to Vice President for Corporate Relations, an important position that keeps him away from the news department.
Then ABC hired Elmer Lower as President of News, Special Events,
and Public Affairs. A reporter for United Press at the beginning of
his career, Lower had moved on to CBS News, then switched to
NBC, where he had a strong hand in the rejuvenation that enabled
NBC to become the leading network news operation. One of his

first moves at ABC was to pay a voice specialist $15,000 to round out the ragged tones of Hagerty's ace reporters.

Ironically, the announcer era of television news had begun to dissolve long before Hagerty went into the business. NBC and CBS had learned two lessons through painful trial and error: The announcer who knows little about news exposes his own incompetence ("giving the listener the spooky feeling," James Thurber wrote, "that the deaths of scores of persons in an air crash are not more important than a new candy bar or brand of coffee"), but the reporter who has no sense of style is also lost. TV news, the more insightful executives had decided, was neither show business nor journalism, but the illegitimate child of both.

And so it is that the network men who have slowly come to the forefront in television news are almost all hybrids. They have, one critic pointed out, "a special and unpredictable combination of face, voice, and attitude which happen, at a particular time, to capture public imagination." They also have years of experience with great events, which was emphasized when CBS brought together six of its on-camera stars to present the special "Years of Progress" program as 1964 began. One had worked for the State Department in Moscow; five were former newspaper reporters.

With few exceptions, the leading TV commentators began as newsmen and retain the reporter's zest for news. Although they must be sensitive to the slender attention span of an audience that always expects a *show*, and hence tend to broadcast small packages of factual drama, most of them are apologetic about it. As Walter Cronkite, who began as a United Press reporter, says resignedly of television news, "It can't be anything but a front-page service. There just isn't enough time to give more than a few headlines and then hope people will read the next morning's paper." Compared to a newspaper, Cronkite holds, any TV news program "is a paltry sideshow."

Significantly, the Washington correspondents reserve their highest enthusiasm for the commentators who are restive with television. First among them is Eric Sevareid, who began as a newspaperman and is so concerned with the course of world events that, according to one who has worked with him: "He gets up in the morning and vomits about what's happening in Berlin." Sevareid has continued with CBS, but he began devoting his best work to a newspaper column after years of grousing about the growing limitations of TV. "The bigger the information media the less courage and freedom of expression they allow," he says, an obvious reference to the current giantism of CBS. Sevareid was happiest with broadcasting during the 1930's and 1940's, when CBS Radio kept a small, brilliant stable of great correspondents. Now he complains, "The most personal form of journalism ever known, in terms of the immediate communicator and the immediate listener, has become depersonalized in its processing stages, so many are the people and the separate functions that become involved."

Edward R. Murrow, whose influence with the correspondents was as great, left broadcasting altogether after several angrily articulate blasts at the network powers. "Surely we shall pay for using this most powerful instrument of communications to insulate the citizenry from the hard and demanding realities which must be faced if we are to survive," Murrow held. "I would like television to produce some itching pills rather than this endless outpouring of tranquilizers."

Howard K. Smith, the incisively intellectual ex-United Press reporter, is a special and revealing case. He left the lucrative and prestigious position of Chief Washington Correspondent for CBS in a dispute over his freedom to comment on events. "On newspapers you have both reporters and columnists," he points out. "There is no reason why that procedure cannot be applied to television." But Smith himself has had trouble applying it. On one of the "News and Comment" programs that he began over ABC after leaving CBS, Smith presented a political obituary of Richard Nixon that included a two-minute interview with Alger Hiss. Nixon himself had devoted much of his political autobiography to the Hiss Case, but there was a prompt rush for the door by several sponsors of *other* ABC programs, apparently on the theory that breaking a contract is better business

than staying in the vicinity of adult reportage. At the end of the
season, Smith's own sponsor deserted him. But the starkest display of
apologetic journalism came from two of the ABC stations that refused to broadcast the program, then blacked out references to it
in the next day's news reports.

Clearly, television has not yet attained the freedom of daily
newspapers, most of which have published thousands of quotations
from Alger Hiss. The news departments of all three networks are
now solidly staffed with crack journalists. Within months, Elmer
Lower had done so much for ABC that the leading television critics
were writing that there were now three network news operations
where before there had been only two worthy of the name. But until
television achieves freedom from its particular fears, most correspondents are likely to continue to view it with lingering unease and
applaud the commentators who are in conflict with it.

It is doubtful that commentators will ever be able to swing with
all the freedom of the newspaper columnists, but that is not likely to
affect the one who is slowly acquiring the greatest influence on the
slowly changing techniques of presenting news on television, David
Brinkley. For although he too, is an ex-reporter (Wilmington, N.C.,
Star-News and United Press) and is sometimes impatient with the
superficial scope of TV, he is one of the few newscasters who range
widely enough to be considered a *commentator*—one who expresses
attitudes toward the news. It is a measure of Brinkley's subtlety that
his commentaries are broadcast by NBC, which was long notable
for neutral tones. And they are subtle expressions indeed, for Brinkley seldom uses "It seems to me," "My opinion," and other baldly
editorial lead-ins, and he never betrays elation or outrage.

It is a slippery task, in fact, to show that Brinkley *is* more than a
newscaster. He never identifies gods and devils as explicitly as does
Radio Commentator Fulton Lewis, Jr. But anyone who watches him
regularly can visualize his gods and devils—and venture confidently
that Brinkley and Fulton Lewis wouldn't get along very well. More
to the point, watching Brinkley, then one of the more conventional

television newsmen—say, Cronkite—makes it clear that Brinkley's presentation of events is a network of nuances. He reacts to the news, often with a tone of irony and the facsimile of a smile.

Although many television critics have hailed the Brinkley style as a refreshing new phenomenon, it has been developing for more than twenty years. Leaving United Press in 1943 to write news scripts for NBC in Washington, Brinkley was encouraged by News Manager William McAndrew to go on radio—"in the early mornings so that nobody would hear me." In 1953, NBC tried him on television, but again at a time (Sundays at noon) when only news addicts would know about it. However, McAndrew and others who considered Brinkley talented were soon high in the NBC councils. In 1956, Brinkley and Chet Huntley, who was already taking shape as the fluent answer to CBS's Ed Murrow, were sent to the national political conventions. Assigned to spell each other, they decided instead to work together. "I did what I'd been doing for years," Brinkley says, "but now people were paying attention."

The nation was so attentive to Brinkley's relaxed irony and so taken by his chemistry with Huntley that NBC immediately set up the "Huntley-Brinkley Report." It built such a strong following that when Huntley and Brinkley returned to the conventions in 1960 they spread-eagled the field, winning 51 per cent of the audience to 36 per cent for CBS and 13 for ABC. In 1964, they nearly doubled the combined audiences of CBS and ABC.

One of the more astute television critics, Robert Lewis Shayon, holds that the "Huntley-Brinkley Report" owes some of its popularity to the fact that Huntley and Brinkley are essentially moralists. Wry commentary is only the frosting; the program is distinctive for the revelatory footnotes that give flesh to facts.

Thinking of Brinkley as a moralist is a great improvement on a more widespread belief: that he is a topical humorist who just happens to be working on a news program rather than on a comedy show. A light edge is often visible, but the stark difference between Brinkley and the wisecrackers is apparent from the difference in the approach of Mort Sahl and the way Brinkley commented on the 1960 conventions.

Sahl suggested that Kennedy should get the nomination because the nation was seeking a "son-figure," and he applauded Kennedy's appearance on College News Conference because "kids like to talk over their problems with someone their own age." He introduced the chief telephone operator of the convention with: "They have good exchanges for a convention—like RUthlessness, AVarice, BLitz, and MAchine." Then he added, "I have only a few months to tell these jokes before they become treason."

Brinkley was on the periphery of wisecracking when he termed the Democratic Convention "the first convention of the space age— where a candidate can promise the moon and mean it," and when he saluted Lyndon Johnson's acceptance of the Vice Presidential nomination with the suggestion that the slogan "All the Way with LBJ" be changed to "Half the Way with LBJ."

But the thrust of Brinkley's appeal is not waggery; it is his mood of inner amusement. "This is the convention," he said on opening day, "and there are those who love it." He described the 1960 Republican Convention as "an honest-to-goodness convention; last time it was a coronation," and said of Senator Everett Dirksen: "When he talks, the words come out distinctly like little rubber balloons filled with helium; they just float up to the ceiling."

The style of Brinkley's commentary is typified by this item from the Huntley-Brinkley Report:

> During today's debate on the nuclear treaty . . . Senator Fulbright of Arkansas said in a speech [that] the human race— if it cared to, as it probably did not—could learn a great deal from the sea gull. This idea was never before presented to the United States Senate . . . and so the other members were slow to react.
>
> Fulbright said that while mankind builds ever bigger bombs, the sea gull has learned to live in peace. If two gulls are really furious at each other . . . he said one of them will reach down with his beak and pull up a few blades of grass, and that's the end of it.
>
> Also, he said, the gull is monogamous, devoted to private

property and as devoted to seniority as even the Senate is.
Well, Fulbright made his point . . . but there is more to it
than that. It is also true the sea gull sits around on the water
waiting for food to float by. He refuses to dive for it. Or, he
will follow behind a ship, waiting for something edible to be
thrown overboard. Or, if that fails, he will find another bird's
nest and steal the eggs.

Perhaps Senator Fulbright did not have all the facts . . . because it is doubtful he would advocate a society in which no one
fights . . . but no one has anything to eat unless it is given to
him or unless he steals it.

This kind of thing has made Brinkley so successful ("a sure
commercial sale," one executive put it) that NBC guarantees him a
minimum of $3,000 a week for the next ten years. As a result, hun-
dreds of television screens that do not carry the Huntley-Brinkley
Report do carry imitations of the distinctive Brinkley style. Many
newscasters have taken to clipping their words in Brinkley's decisive
way and try to add a touch of wry humor to at least one item in each
program. They usually fail because, as a former NBC man points
out, "The secret of his success is his ability to be humorous in a
few words. He writes very economically. Harry Reasoner and Bob
Trout of CBS try to match him. But they start from the 50-yard line,
and by the time they get to the goal, their attempted humor is too
labored. Brinkley can do it from inside the 20."

Like Walter Lippmann, who admires Brinkley as "one who
knows what's going on," Brinkley is not a reporter in the conventional sense. He seldom goes out and digs for news, preferring to
concentrate on writing. He is intensely proud that he writes every
word that he says on the air. And so it is that, like Lippmann, Brinkley tends to raise the level of prose in the Washington press corps
and lower the level of reporting. Other television newsmen—and not
a few of the newspaper and magazine correspondents—are inclined
by his example to shun the digging for hard facts and to concentrate
on shaping into tasty capsules the news gathered by others. The

danger is that the journalist who is divorced from news gathering, who has not faced the public official and asked him the pointed question, may be lured, by a desire to write bright passages, into sacrificing facts for phrases.

It is difficult to say whether Brinkley would be a more satisfactory model for other correspondents if he were to devote more time to reporting and less to writing. The Washington press corps must have high standards in both categories, and it is doubtful that a daily commentator can chase news through the labyrinths of the Capital and still have time to write it compellingly.

It is nonetheless easy to suspect that another NBC star of lesser magnitude, John Chancellor, who need not prepare a daily news show, is a better model for the average correspondent. A bright writer and an arresting personality, Chancellor has a dedication of a single-minded kind to the fundamentals of journalism. Once, he was making $100,000 a year running the "Today" show. But to keep the job, he was told that he would have to read commercials as well as news. He quit and went back to reporting.

CHAPTER SIX

TIME and Pearson:
The Influence of the "Outcasts"

Letter to the Editor of *Time:*

Sir:

In addition to eight quotations torn out of context, your recent article on me contained no less than seven more or less gross errors of fact. As the article began by getting my name wrong, and finished by getting my weight wrong, it would be too time-consuming to attempt to correct all the errors, one by one. But I must at least correct *Time*'s story of my reason for choosing my brother as my partner. I asked my brother to be my partner because I knew he wrote admirably, because I was sure he would be a first-class reporter, and because I could not think of anyone else with these essential assets who did not already have a bigger job than I could offer. Whoever put into my mouth the pretentious damfool statement that I chose Stew because he was "the only writer . . . one would not throw out of one's rooms," was a liar, and in my opinion a malicious liar.   JOSEPH ALSOP

"Washington Merry-Go-Round," October 11, 1964: "Some new angles have developed in the Justice

Department's trial of Teamster boss Jimmy Hoffa. . . .

"The evidence shows that Bobby Kennedy deliberately planted a story with Life magazine regarding Hoffa, timed to break before his trial in Nashville.

". . . the Justice Department surrounded the jurors with a group of rowdy U.S. marshals who indulged in heavy drinking and made the floor of the hotel where they were locked up a virtual night-club. . . ."

U.S. Department of Justice Statement: "In this column, Mr. Pearson presents as new 'evidence' charges which were made by Mr. Hoffa and his co-defendants some seven months ago.

"He fails to note that all of these allegations, including the affidavits from which he quotes, were presented to the United States District Court in Chattanooga seven months ago and are part of the public record.

"Mr. Pearson also fails to note that the Government introduced considerable testimony refuting these allegations, and that after considering both sides, Judge Frank W. Wilson totally rejected the accusations."

A Washington correspondent who takes pride in the profession of reporting will almost certainly develop a hate-love relationship with the most widely circulated news magazine, *Time*, and the most widely syndicated political columnist, Drew Pearson. The hatred is easy to explain. In the words of one correspondent, *"Time* and Pearson are often in error but never in doubt." Others are vehement, declaring that the "errors" that appear in *Time* and in Pearson's "Washington Merry-Go-Round" are not errors at all but intentional distortions. Both the magazine and the column, it is said, debase the currency of political journalism by making everything that comes out of Washington suspect.

Ralph Ingersoll, a former publisher of *Time*, lends support, saying of its methods: "The way to tell a successful lie is to include enough truth in it to make it believable—and *Time* is the most successful liar of our times." T. S. Matthews, who worked for the magazine for twenty-four years and eventually became its editor, has written that "the presidential campaign of 1940 was the last one that *Time* even tried to report fairly. . . . In 1952, when it sniffed victory in the air at last, there was no holding *Time*. The distortions, suppressions and slanting of its political 'news' seemed to me to pass the bounds of politics and to commit an offense against the ethics of journalism."

No critic who has ever gone seriously about the business of tracing bias in *Time* has lacked evidence. Milton Gwirtzman, one of the most incisive critics, demonstrated the magazine's Republican bias by matching its attitudes toward the same subjects under Democratic and Republican administrations. When the Democrats controlled the Executive branch in 1952, *Time* ruminated: "This week, once again, the American taxpayer . . . was working over his income tax return. He did not do the job happily. . . . The blow, in full and crushing measure, now lands each March 15 on the chin of a fellow named John Q." But under a Republican Administration, *Time* reported in its issue of April 18, 1955: ". . . 60 million Americans have by this week signed their income tax forms. . . . They did this, wonderful to tell, without riots or protest. . . . It has become more and more unfashionable to criticize the income tax level."

Gwirtzman also showed how a Democrat's character changes dramatically in *Time* when he begins to associate with Republicans.

When George E. Allen was a close friend of President Truman, *Time* judged: "George is all the more remarkable because, to the naked eye, he is a clown." And when Truman apponted Allen to the Board of Directors of the Reconstruction Finance Corporation, *Time* called him the President's "croniest crony." But when Allen moved with the Republican tide in the elections of 1952 and became one of President Eisenhower's closest friends, *Time* was suddenly respectful: "Last week the President chatted quietly with . . . golfing companion George E. Allen, Washington lawyer and friend of Presidents."

Time has twisted its judgments to suit its biases across an astonishing range of subjects. Under Truman, when the Consumer Price Index went up to 183.8: "Never in U.S. history had the cost of living been so high." But when, under Eisenhower, the Index was nearly 9 points higher at 192.3: ". . . the U.S. is more prosperous than ever before." When Truman refused during a press conference to say whether he would run for re-election 1952, *Time* labeled his responses "deliberately mysterious . . . a stale joke." But when Eisenhower did the same, *Time* reported: "Adroitly, he fielded the questions." Innuendo greeted the President's travels across the country during the Truman days: "Officially, the trip will be billed as non-political, an ancient device whereby a President can pay his expenses from his $40,000 travel allowance instead of from the party treasury." But *Time* considered political jaunts a national benefit under Eisenhower: "From time to time, a President of the United States must travel around the country."

Pearson's bias tilts him in the other direction, but it is no less flagrant. Although he has earned the enmity of some Democratic Presidents and has often attacked Democrats in Congress, the preponderance of his columns favor Democratic liberals. Douglass Cater, long one of the most serious and respected correspondents, and himself a liberal, says of Pearson: "His phenomenal inaccuracy with names, dates, places, and the other elemental details of reporting casts suspicion on everything he writes." During the Eisenhower Presidency, another correspondent asserted, "You could count on

Pearson attacking the President every other day—sometimes with facts."

Pearson's fancies included a long, fuzzy column on an imaginary Eisenhower "relapse" after an illness and a fantastic report asserting that Vice President Nixon had tried to seize the reins of government while the President was ill (the very last action Nixon could take and hope to succeed Eisenhower in the Presidency). During the Kennedy Era, Pearson reminisced in a column on Presidential news management about the time when Eisenhower's Press Secretary James Hagerty had managed the headlines in 1954 by rushing out an announcement "that Mr. Eisenhower planned to launch a new satellite into outer space." This would have been three years before the first satellite was launched.

Time and the "Washington Merry-Go-Round" get such low marks for reliability that it is tempting to conclude that they have approximately the same influence on the press corps that Barry Goldwater has on Americans for Democratic Action. But there are reasons for doubting that they are quite the outcasts they seem.

Neither *Time* nor Pearson can be dismissed lightly, for in the privacy of their homes and offices, most correspondents are avid readers of both. Asked to name the magazines he reads regularly, James Reston listed a long string that began with *Newsweek* and ended with *The Reporter*. Pressed to say whether he reads others, Reston responded a bit grudgingly, "And, of course, the Luce magazines, *Time* and the rest." Another correspondent who dislikes *Time* intensely confessed that he could not bear to miss an issue. He paid for a subscription, then discovered that he could get each issue a day earlier at the National Press Building newsstand. Unable to wait for his subscription copy, he began picking it up at the newsstand. "Then," he said, "I cuss my way through it. It's simplified and slanted —and I read every word."

As for the "Washington Merry-Go-Round," nearly every correspondent will admit reading it daily because, as one pointed out, "You never can tell when it's going to carry the best story out of Washington." The real essence of the correspondents' attitude toward Pearson may have been expressed in a "T.R.B." column in *The New Republic:* "Half a dozen of us at lunch at the Press Club last week were talking about Drew Pearson's recent columns on the Catholic hierarchy. 'Let's face it,' one reporter said finally, 'not one of us here would have the nerve to write what Pearson does, or hope to get it printed!' Nobody denied it."

The truth is that the Washington correspondents react to *Time* and to Pearson with the same suspicious but hypnotized attention that is so notable among other critics. Many academicians are caustic about all Time, Inc., publications—a Harvard savant dismisses *Life* and *Time* as "one for those who can't read and the other for those who can't think"—but professors and their students subscribe in such numbers that *Time* is the most widely read magazine on most college campuses. One professor of philosophy, a noted Kantian, shares with his wife an addiction to *Time* so acute that they sometimes tear it in half down the binding, so that neither will have an agonizing wait. As for Pearson, he is supposedly dismissed everywhere as wildly inaccurate, but social scientists share his suspicion of big-business power so completely that Congressional assistants say that the "Merry-Go-Round" inspires more of the Why-don't-you-do-something-about-this? mail from outraged professors than any other column.

It is the same in government. The boast of Bureau Chief John Steele that Washington officials "read the hell out of *Time*" is quite true—even among those who dislike it. John Kennedy had little reason to love *Time*, which supported Nixon in 1960 and treated Kennedy, at best, with barbed respect. Among other indignities, *Time* reported that Kennedy had received a "cool reception" in North Dakota when, in fact, 25,000 had gathered to hear him speak —a huge throng in a state whose population is only nine to the square mile. But Kennedy considered *Time* the most important magazine in America; it reaches the kind of people a political leader must influence. He got his copy early every week and was usually on the telephone to White House Correspondent Hugh Sidey within an hour, sometimes with praise, usually with complaints. Kennedy once said, somewhat despairingly, that when he asked foreign leaders who exhibited detailed knowledge of U.S. affairs where they got their information, they invariably answered, "In *Time.*"

Pearson's effect on officialdom is more direct. As *Time* once reported: "His is the kind of journalistic vigilance that keeps small men honest; and forces bigger men to work in an atmosphere of caution that frequently cramps their style." Pearson's revelations have sent four Members of Congress to jail, defeated countless others, and caused the dismissal of scores of government officials. His digging covers a wide range—from evidence that Congressman Andrew May of Kentucky took a bribe to evidence that a State Department official leaked documents to the Senate. Almost anything that smacks of wrongdoing is likely to get a wild ride on the "Merry-Go-Round." Pearson was responsible for the firing of James B. Cash, Jr., Deputy Commissioner of the Federal Housing Administration. The "Merry-Go-Round" reported that Cash had lost $7,000 in a blackjack game at a builders' convention, and he was promptly dismissed. Pearson is "vicious"—a description offered by California Secretary of State Frank Jordan, who won an apology and a retraction from Pearson after filing a $1-million libel suit against him. Or he is "one of the best inspectors general"—which was the view of General George C. Marshall. The dismaying part for those who try to assess his worth— the Washington *Post* has long debated in high executive councils whether to discontinue his column or give it a more prominent place —is that both are probably accurate.

No one in Washington can afford to ignore either *Time* or Pearson for one reason: Despite biases and distortions, they are the most *affecting* reporters of politics at work today.

Time's reportage attracts readers because it is clever, crisp, and evocative.* It is persuasive because the writers make convincing use

---

* One newspaper correspondent keeps close at hand a booklet entitled "A Matter of Manner," which is made up of excerpts from some of *Time*'s brighter stories. The correspondent reads it immediately before beginning his own writing, hoping that some of its brisk, visual prose will rub off on his own stories. One of the items: "The old man puffed into sight like a venerable battle wagon steaming up over the horizon. First a smudge of smoke, then the long cigar, then the famil-

of detail. Thus, *Time* once reported that a press secretary argued with the President about the way press conferences were going. But the argument was not recounted in straightforward fact. Instead, the press secretary "left his pale green office, walked thirty brisk steps down the hall, opened the door, and took seven more paces to the desk of the President of the U.S." Any reader who might have doubted that any such argument ever took place is convinced by those thirty brisk steps and seven more paces, which paralyze the critical faculties.

In less adept hands, this technique is a parody of itself. And in fact, one former *Time* editor has admitted that, after floundering during his early days with the magazine, he succeeded by consciously burlesquing its style. But, handled dexterously, *Time* trivia is persuasion of a highly convincing kind—the Truth According to Trivial Detail. Given unexpected and precise bits of information in a cleverly written chronicle, readers unconsciously assume that the entire melange is made up of inside truths. Thus, in one of its more convincing stories on John Kennedy, *Time* reported that he had "leaned across the asparagus" at a dinner party to ask Jackie for their first date. Whether the item had any relevance to anything significant was not important; readers unwittingly accepted it as another evidence of *Time*'s omniscience and were less inclined to doubt the part of the story that was significant.

This technique was especially useful during the Eisenhower years, when *Time*'s favorite President had a press secretary, James Hagerty, with the wit to understand its implications. When Eisenhower was knocked flat by rumbles in head, heart, and stomach and the fearful were saying their prayers and selling their stocks, Hagerty was quick to announce that the President had broth, creamed cabbage, and a bacon-lettuce-and-tomato sandwich for lunch and an anticoagulant afterward. The important matter was not the medication but the itemized menu. Later, announcements about Eisen-

---

iar, stoop-shouldered hulk that a generation had come to know as the silhouette of greatness. Prime Minister Winston Churchill scowled as . . ." Like some other bright items in *Time*, this is a shaky analogy. Surely the first sight of a man like Churchill takes in his bulk, not the smoke from his cigar.

hower's bowel movements made all other questions redundant. It is difficult to ask for much more truth about a Presidential illness when one has been led vicariously into his bathroom.

Time and Hagerty were responsible for one of the most notable triumphs of convincing trivia. This came in December, 1957, when President Eisenhower suffered a stroke. Hagerty was then in Paris, and Associate Press Secretary Anne Wheaton—who had taken over temporarily with the proud comment, "I am not a panic person"— panicked. She first identified the stroke as "a form of heart attack," then amended, "Cerebral does have something to do with the head." Worse, she did not report on the President's diet or regularity. Some of Eisenhower's firmest friends in the press corps began to speculate in print about the possibility of an Eisenhower resignation.

Then *Time* and Hagerty took over. "Back from Paris," *Time* recounted, "Old Reporter Hagerty breezed into his first press conference next morning with clear-cut answers and a passel of tidbits such as his report that Ike had shaved himself (safety razor) and had eaten a hearty breakfast (grapefruit, creamed chipped beef, toast and honey, Sanka)." This trivia almost did its work too well; Hagerty soon found himself protesting to some suddenly optimistic reporters that the medical case on Eisenhower's illness was not closed just because Eisenhower was planning to attend church the following Sunday.

Although the texture of Pearson's prose is not nearly so smooth and clever as *Time*'s, the contrast is not entirely detrimental. The "Merry-Go-Round" is more persuasive for many readers *because* it reads, as one critic has said, "like jottings on an envelope in a lurching taxicab." There is in Pearson's ragged writing (and in some of the newsletters) a suggestion of the aura of the reporter whose passion for presenting inside facts transcends the niceties of composition.

More important, Pearson is aware that paraphrase is only minimally persuasive. He reproduces telephone dialogues, knowing that the appeal of pointed question-and-answer testimony is not limited to courtrooms. Others write *about* confidential memoranda. Pearson's method is illustrated by his actions when he pried loose memos showing that Congressman Albert Thomas of Texas had used his

influence with the National Space Agency to have a lucrative contract awarded to Southern Bell Telephone. The "Merry-Go-Round"
printed them in full.

Pearson makes a fetish of exact quotations, and when he does
not have them, he re-creates them. Shortly after Lyndon Johnson
entered the White House, much of one "Merry-Go-Round" was
devoted to a jocular colloquy involving the President, Press Secretary
Pierre Salinger, and Senator Hubert Humphrey:

> "Pierre," said Mr. Johnson accusingly, "you are beginning
> to look like a candidate. So many pictures of you are appearing
> in the papers that it looks as if you are running for vice presi-
> dent."
>
> This brought a mock protest from Senator Hubert Humphrey
> (Dem.-Minn.), who charged that the White House was favoring
> other vice presidential candidates over him, Humphrey. It had
> assumed the proportions of a conspiracy, he said.
>
> "Sargent Shriver (Peace Corps director) has taken a message
> from you to the Pope," Humphrey reminded the President.
> "Bobby Kennedy (attorney general) has been dispatched to the
> Far East to save the peace. . . . What have you done for
> Humphrey?"

This exchange came during a meeting of the President with
Congressional leaders in the White House conference room. No journalist was on hand. Pearson's report was accurate in substance—a
columnist syndicated by six hundred newspapers can coax government officials into revealing a great deal. But the direct quotations
create the impression that Drew Pearson is behind every closed door.

How far Pearson will go to convince his readers of the authenticity of his reports is shown in his account of an Eisenhower campaign trip in 1956. Pearson was informed by a usually reliable source
in Minneapolis that Eisenhower had suffered a mild relapse. The
"Merry-Go-Round" of the following day reported that Eisenhower
had been stricken again and that his car had pulled out of the campaign entourage. Films that had been taken at the time proved that

nothing of the sort had occurred. So far, this would have been only an erroneous report, springing from a mistake made by a customarily reliable source. But Pearson went much further, writing of the President: "He suddenly turned to the others in the car and announced, 'I can't take any more of this. Let's get out of here.' "

Time spends $5 million a year to maintain correspondents in all the world capitals, a sizable fraction of it to operate the Washington Bureau, which is by far its largest. (By press corps standards, *Time*'s Washington offices are plush and its employees well paid.) What a correspondent for *Time* must do is outlined in a manual for its reporters which emphasizes writing style, then adds:

"Far more important is that you tell us all we need to know, not merely to get the key facts straight but to see, feel, hear—even smell—what has happened.

"What color and texture were the dress?

"How did the mayor enter the editor's office?

"Exactly what did the druggist say to the narcotics agent?

"Of what kind of wood was the doctor's table made?"

Thus, *Time*'s correspondents are concerned not only with the substance of the press conference and the speech and the Senate debate but also with the manner of the speaker, the color of the drapes, and what the press secretary whispered to the President. More than any other correspondents, *Time*'s men must re-create the atmosphere and the flavor of news.

Every Washington correspondent for *Time* soon becomes aware that he is not a reporter in the conventional sense. As one editor has said, "The first difference between *Time*'s Washington coverage and that of other big news publications is this: *Time*'s correspondents don't write directly for the readers of *Time*, but for *Time*'s editors." The correspondents write endless reports—those for a cover story on Secretary of Agriculture Freeman totaled more than 45,000 words —but seldom see any of their own words in print. One story, perhaps apocryphal, tells of the *Time* correspondent who came into the office one day gesturing excitedly at a line in a new issue. "Look, I got something in," he said. "That's mine—that *comma*, right there!"

The frustrations of the middleman journalist are many. It is difficult, first, for a correspondent with average pride to work anonymously, especially when other correspondents reap daily by-lines. It is worse to interview high officials and then to see your report twisted on publication. More than one *Time* correspondent in Washington has saved carbon copies to prove that the distortions came later in the editorial process. On occasion, too, relations between *Time* correspondents and the rest of the press corps have become ragged because an official who has been roasted in *Time* develops a suspicion of all journalists. One such occasion came in 1961 when Congressman John J. Rooney, the powerful chairman of the House subcommittee that largely determines the size and shape of the State Department's budget, refused to speak to any journalist for weeks. *Time* had parboiled him.

Such frustrations are largely responsible for the changes in *Time*'s Washington Bureau. Only one correspondent who was reporting for *Time* from Washington ten years ago is still on the job—John L. Steele, who was then covering Congress and is now Bureau Chief. (Curiously, *Time*'s Washington Bureau Chiefs during the past fifteen years have almost uniformly enjoyed the liking and respect of most officials and correspondents. Beginning with Felix Belair, who rejoined the New York *Times* Bureau after several years with *Time* as Bureau Chief, and extending through the present, only James Shepley does not qualify. Shepley was able, a former *Time* executive explained, "but they couldn't keep him in Washington after he wrote that article on John Foster Dulles' brinkmanship.") A few former correspondents have moved to other work within Time, Inc. "By the time you're sick of working for this operation you're making too much money to leave," one explained, but most have joined other publications. One who moved on, Tom Lambert of the New York *Herald Tribune*, says, "You get tired of not being able to control your own copy."

What sometimes happens is revealed by an intramural fight over *Time*'s coverage of Vietnam. Charles Mohr, who was long the White House correspondent for *Time*, was sent to Southeast Asia as chief correspondent. For months, Mohr had been filing reports from Saigon, showing that the Diem government was shaky and that the war with the Communists was not going well. But *Time*'s editors altered the reports to minimize Diem's failings, and even twisted them to indicate that he was winning. Finally, Mohr wrote flatly that "the war is being lost," a conclusion which had been reached by the other American correspondents on the scene. Managing Editor Otto Fuerbringer not only junked Mohr's report, he set out to counter similar reports that were then appearing in other magazines and newspapers. A young contributing editor, Gregory Dunne, was assigned to the task. He refused. Other editors then fashioned a story aptly summarized by one of its phrases, "government soldiers are fighting better than ever."

Fuerbringer went further. He called in a writer and dictated the substance of an attack on all American correspondents in Vietnam. Before this could appear in the magazine, Richard Clurman, chief of *Time* correspondents, tried to call Henry Luce, the only editor who could overrule Fuerbringer. But Luce was in Atlanta at a football game.

The attack on the correspondents was published. That was enough for Mohr, who said that he would resign unless he were given a column of space in *Time* to refute it. Clurman knew this would be impossible, but he flew from his Paris headquarters to New York to confer with Luce.

It was a sticky situation for Luce. He admired Clurman and Mohr, but he did not want to censure his managing editor. He tried to compromise, directing Clurman and Mohr to fly to Saigon and write a "corrective" story. Fearing the worst if another report on the press in Saigon were sent through Fuerbringer's editing mill, Clurman argued against another story. Luce insisted. Clurman's fears proved well grounded. When the "corrective" was published, one of the offended correspondents simply considered it a sequel to the first injury. "Both pieces could have been written by Madame Nhu," he said. Mohr quit and was promptly hired by the New York *Times*.

In theory, anonymity is also the rule for Drew Pearson's staff of three reporters. But Jack Anderson, Pearson's handsome chief assistant and heir apparent, is hardly anonymous. Not only does Pearson occasionally turn over the "Merry-Go-Round" to him, usually with a proud note that "today's column is written by my junior partner," but Anderson has sometimes been a central figure in Washington events. During the memorable Congressional investigation of the influence of Bernard Goldfine on Eisenhower's Presidential assistant Sherman Adams, Anderson was caught bugging Goldfine's suite in the Sheraton-Carlton Hotel. (Electronic eavesdropping works both ways. Government officials once put so many telephone taps on the lines between Pearson's home and that of an assistant that they could hardly hear each other.)

More recently, Anderson himself was the subject of an investigation. He had written an exposé of Congressional cheating on expense accounts and profiteering on government land contracts. Congressman Omar Burleson angrily announced an investigation when he saw the by-line: "By an Anonymous Congressman as Told to Jack Anderson." After Anderson was sworn in as a witness, Burleson gestured toward the telephone, which had been specially installed, and said, "I am ready to call a member of the House or the Senate whom you name as your informant in order that he or she may confront you here and now. Will you name that member?" Anderson refused. The hearing suddenly became a shouting contest. Incensed by the support for Anderson among the correspondents covering the hearing, a burly Congressman invited a correspondent to settle the argument man-to-man. Sarah McClendon added to the confusion by yelling, apparently at everyone, "What are you trying to hide here?" Burleson adjourned the hearing. Anderson held a press conference.

Pearson seems to prize flamboyance in his chief assistants. Anderson's predecessor was David Karr, who was surely one of the brashest correspondents who ever covered Washington. One of the first to have a telephone installed in his automobile, Karr often called government secretaries and asked them to run to the window and wave to him as he drove by. He claims an I.Q. of 189—about fifty points above the threshold of genius. Before moving into the business world (in 1959 he became the president of Fairbanks, Whitney), Karr was earning $20,000 a year working for the "Merry-Go-Round" though not yet thirty years old. And Pearson, although he indicates that Karr remembers his own role a bit too positively, remembers his former aide affectionately: "Dave had the faculty of being a salesman. Most people don't think of a newspaperman as being a salesman, but he has to persuade people to talk, persuade them to hand over important documents."

Karr's persuasiveness is almost legendary. When Henry J. Kaiser boiled into Pearson's office one day to complain about an item, Karr charmed him so effectively that they became close friends and swapped information. Later, when Karr and Pearson were jointly distributing a newsletter called *Personal from Pearson*, Karr regularly gleaned facts from unpublished memos that *Time*'s Washington staff sent to the magazine's editors in New York.

Salesmanship, of a sort, is still the basis of many columns. Pearson operates on a system of rewards and punishments. The public official who displeases him can expect rough rides on the "Merry-Go-Round"—a fact of which Senator Robert Kennedy is now well aware. But those who share Pearson's prejudices, and especially those who supply secret information, are rewarded with favorable mention. For years before his death, Senator Estes Kefauver of Tennessee served Pearson, and himself, by disclosing what went on behind closed doors in the Senate. Now, it is widely said that President Johnson has become Pearson's best source. It is even suspected by some correspondents that the Administration official who turned over to Pearson documents casting doubt on the veracity of an unfriendly witness in the Bobby Baker case was the President himself.

Pearson maintains that most of his information is developed from tips supplied by patriotic Americans: "There are an awful lot of citizens in the United States who are for good government, and they send me tips." This is beyond question; Pearson and his staff spend much of their time trying to develop big stories from small tips. It is also true that Pearson's assistants usually avoid off-the-record conferences, preferring to pump the correspondents who do attend them and are unable to use their information. And in Washington and abroad there are correspondents who do not actually work for Pearson, but who turn over to him leads to stories that they cannot develop adequately.

The one certainty, according to correspondents who know Pearson well, is that he is absolutely fearless, and the best investigator in Washington.

Time's editorial chairman, Henry Luce, may be the strangest press lord in the history of American journalism (as well as the first to earn that identity through magazine publishing alone). Born in 1898 to American missionaries in China, he has long been insatiably curious. Graduated from Yale in 1920 as the "most brilliant" student in his class, he and the graduate who was voted "most likely to succeed," Briton Hadden, brought out the first issue of *Time* in 1923 and served alternately as editor and business manager, changing every six months. Four years later, the magazine was making money. In 1929, the year Hadden died, the company was strong enough to launch *Fortune*. In 1936, *Life* was born, and almost immediately became one of the most popular magazines in the world. In 1964, when many another magazine empire was shaky, Time, Inc., reported record earnings of $26,526,000—a gain of 87 per cent over 1963. This seems to be the continuing success story of an editorial genius, and yet the estimates of Luce by his long-time associates make it difficult to understand any of his triumphs. He has always been, one says, "a chaotic man." Margaret Bourke-White, the first *Fortune* photographer, has described Luce on their first meeting in 1929: "He was perhaps a year or two under thirty, strikingly powerful in build, with a large head over large shoulders. His words tumbled out with such haste and emphasis that I had the feeling he was thinking ten words for every one that managed to emerge." Luce's inability to co-ordinate thought and speech has been so much a part of his life that T. S. Matthews says flatly, "He's incoherent." Even a Time, Inc., biography describes Luce, somewhat cautiously, as one who "sometimes stutters and hesitates."

There are other paradoxes. Luce is religious to the point of other-worldliness—and at the same time notably tough-minded. His magazines are dedicated to flushing out secrets and publicizing them, yet Luce himself is secretive and fearful of personal publicity. His biases sometimes seem absolute, but when a *Time* reviewer heralded one of Mrs. Luce's plays with graceful words, Luce himself sent the review back for a more honest assessment. His magazines are beautifully organized structures, but during the years when Luce took over as managing editor, he invariably blundered. A little battery of push buttons on the desk of the *Time* managing editor that was designed to summon specialists individually simply would not serve Luce in his more frenetic moments; he pushed all the buttons at once. T. S. Matthews has recalled: "Luce would plan a makeup for the magazine on Thursday, revise it with renewed enthusiasm on Friday, and so on until the ineluctable reality of the waiting presses on Monday night forced a final decision. These constant changes of plan, calling for sketches of layouts, special pictures, maps and ideas for stories, etc., sent everyone scurrying in all directions, doing twice as much work as usual—or as necessary, for at least half of these schemes came to nothing. In the midst of this windy chaos, at its very height, about midnight on Saturday, he would put on his hat and go home. Later stayers had to rescue or create some sort of order out of the gaseous genesis he left behind him."

In short, it is difficult to conceive of a man and a magazine as dissimilar as Luce—serious, disorganized, and indecisive—and *Time* —glib, smooth, and know-it-all.

It is nonetheless clear that much of *Time*'s power and certainty spring from Luce's sense of mission, which former Time, Inc., writer Dwight MacDonald says is "to improve his fellow men." Luce feels that he is carrying out his mission through his magazines. He considers them fair and truthful, although not impartial; the prospectus for *Time* held that journalistic objectivity is not possible and that the new magazine would decide controversial issues by judging which side had the greater merit. In politics, the Republicans are almost always judged to be the most meritorious, but Luce has been known to flame over charges of distortion. He once asked an editor who was quitting *Time* in disgust, "By what right do you put me on the moral defensive?"

Luce's air of moral rightness permeates the upper echelons of Time, Inc. Even those who, like Matthews, have left with a residue of bitterness retain a curious respect, and sometimes even affection, for Henry Luce. Those whose political leanings correspond to Luce's are likely to dismiss criticism the way Chairman of the Board Andrew Heiskell did in a recent speech: "All writers slant what they write no matter how hard they try. All readers slant what they read. If the slants are the same, the magazine is called unbiased. If not, it's accused of bias."

It would be difficult to conceive of a more comfortable attitude.

The similarities between Luce and Drew Pearson are almost as striking as their differences. Like Luce, Pearson is strongly religious; his Quaker rectitude is a clear match for Luce's unflinching Presbyterianism. Both are fervently patriotic and internationalist. And although Pearson considers his role to be that of a "watchdog of government"—several cuts below Luce's dream of the influence of his publishing empire—Pearson is like Luce in the missionary zeal with which he pursues it.

The greatest difference is in personal deportment. Pearson's personality is best revealed by his self-conscious reactions to his own notoriety. When Harry Truman labeled him with a name that almost anyone else would have tried to forget, Pearson played it up in a series of articles in *The Saturday Evening Post:* "Confessions of an S.O.B." When a U.S. Senator who had been attacked in the "Merry-Go-Round" took to the Senate floor and called Pearson an infamous liar, a revolving liar, a pusillanimous liar, a lying ass, a natural-born liar, a liar by profession, a liar for a living, a liar in the daytime, and a liar at night, Pearson reprinted the speech in apparent delight.

Pearson's self-promotion extends even to his errors. On several occasions he has published lengthy corrections of his own false reports, and always in a way that suggests that he has the ultimate power to decide wrongdoing. In eight "I"-studded paragraphs, Pearson once described in detail how he had attacked Senator Frank Lausche of Ohio, then had studied Lausche's financial records and decided the column had been a mistake. Handing down a decision that Lausche was clean after all, he ended the column, "This above all, to thine own self be true. . . ."

It is easy to suspect that almost everything about Pearson's public personality is a pose, including the photograph that many newspapers publish with his column. He is a big, fat man with fringes of white hair. In the quiet of his Georgetown office he is more acidic than egoistic, more likely to slash at his enemies than to promote himself. His principal enemies are not grafting politicians but the editors who publish his column. "They hack it up and twist it around," he complained. "In 1960, I had a lot of brand-new stuff on Nixon, but every California paper except two cut it. And when I asked them why, they said they didn't want any more complaints than they already had from readers. Hell, one editor said he likes my columns better than Lippmann's because mine are easier to cut."

Ironically, a correspondent who is critical of both *Time* and Pearson may provide the most useful assessment of them. "Sometimes I try to imagine what political journalism would be like without them," he said. "I always end up happy that they're here."

It is not an easy conclusion to dismiss. Without *Time*, millions of Americans who formerly bypassed the dreary succession of fact that was once the heart of political journalism would not have been awakened to the zest of politics. Without *Time*, there would have been no *Newsweek*—a fair-minded and fast-improving magazine— for *Time* is responsible for *Newsweek* in the way that all innovators are responsible for their imitators. And without *Time*, a generation of American journalists might not have learned quite so well how to seek out the shape, the color, and the meaning of news, and how to provide the perspective of history.

Without Pearson, Congressmen who richly deserved the prison terms his investigations brought them might have gone unjailed. And an uncountable number of other officials whose depredations were turned up in the "Merry-Go-Round" might have continued careers

of doubtful legality. Without Pearson, political journalism would
not have quite so strong a focus on guarding the public interest, for
many a young correspondent has learned from him how to probe
beneath the surface of government.

Perhaps above all, *Time* and Pearson, for all their biases and
distortions, are fortunate counterweights. One or the other is at least
51 per cent opposed to almost any Administration. And in an era
of government by publicity, every administration needs opposition.

CHAPTER SEVEN

The News Managers—I

"If you even hint where you got it, I'll say you are a damned liar."
—President THEODORE ROOSEVELT after leaking news to three correspondents

"And when Franklin Roosevelt lectures the press, as he does very often, he ascribes its sins to columnists, editors and publishers, implying that the spot-news reporters are fine fellows."
—ARTHUR KROCK

EVER so gradually, the American people are becoming aware of a fact that every President since Washington has either known instinctively or has learned, sometimes too late: Control of information is central to power. Perhaps public awareness began in 1953 with the publication of a private exultation of a White House assistant: "We're going to merchandise the hell out of the Eisenhower Administration!" This was translated into such persistent propaganda for eight years that Joseph Alsop declared as the Eisenhower Presidency was coming to an end: "All government handouts lie; some lie more than others." Awareness certainly grew during the Kennedy Administration, especially when a high official defended his lies to the Washington correspondents with: "News is a weapon in the cold war like any other weapon." Under the Eisenhower, Kennedy, and Johnson systems of government by publicity, news has been a weapon in peace as well. Lacking legal controls over the Washington correspondents, Executive officials have tried to manage the flow of information with threats and favors, silence and oratory, with lies and varying degrees of truth.

There is a more compelling reason for this than simply the desire to create an attractive image. If the Executive branch is to balance the power of Congress, then Executive officials must make themselves the principal source of news and explanation. As Senator J. W.

Fulbright has pointed out, Members of Congress are almost creatures of the press. The cannier Congressmen battle the Executive by playing the press like a symphony orchestra. How far they will go is emphasized by this letter of instructions, which was circulated among members of a House investigating committee:

1. Decide what you want the newspapers to hit hardest and then shape each hearing so that the main point becomes the vortex of the testimony. Once that vortex is reached, *adjourn*.

2. In handling press releases, first put a release date on them, reading something like this: "For release at 10:00 AM EST July 6," etc. If you do this, you can give releases out as much as 24 hours in advance, thus enabling reporters to study them and write better stories.

3. Limit the number of people authorized to speak for the committee, to give out press releases or to provide the press with information to the *smallest number possible*. It plugs leaks and helps preserve the concentration of purpose.

4. Do not permit distractions to occur, such as extraneous fusses with would-be witnesses, which might provide news that would bury the testimony you want featured.

5. Do not space hearings more than 24 hours or 48 hours apart when on a controversial subject. This gives the opposition too much opportunity to make all kinds of counter-charges and replies by issuing statements to the press.

6. Don't ever be afraid to recess a hearing for even five minutes, so that you can keep the proceedings completely in control so far as creating news is concerned.

7. *And this is most important:* don't let the hearings or the evidence ever descend to the plane of a personal fight between the Committee Chairman and the head of the agency being investigated. The high plane of a duly authorized Committee of the House of Representatives *examining* the operations of an Agency of the Executive Branch for constructive purposes should be maintained at all costs.

That the Executive is equally devoted to playing the press is suggested by this confidential memorandum circulated through the Department of Commerce:

> At a White House meeting of Cabinet assistants, we have been advised again that speeches of Cabinet and sub-Cabinet officers do not contain sufficient reference to the President and his personal interest in and compassion with the problems which face the nation. Liberal quotations from his speeches, past and present, should be used.
>
> The above was not deemed to be a reflection on the speeches delivered by Commerce Department officials, but was in the nature of a general comment on all Executive Departments.
>
> It is to be kept in mind that, in making announcements of local projects, the President should be given a credit in the lead paragraph.

Thus Congress and the Executive demonstrate their awareness of a significant fact: Whether the American system is to be defined as Presidential or Congressional government depends largely on whether the President or Congress controls the avenues of information and opinion. And thus the Washington correspondents are caught between factions of government. Managing the news is one of the arts of statecraft.

Modern news management began with Franklin Roosevelt. He did not have the kind of party organ that ground out propaganda for Washington, Jefferson, and Jackson. He did have Lincoln's sense of timing. Lincoln waited for two months for the propitious moment to announce the Emancipation Proclamation. He wrote later: "Finally, came the week of the battle of Antietam. I determined to wait no longer. The news came on Wednesday that the advantage was on our side. . . . The Proclamation was published the following Monday." Similarly, the stunning First Hundred Days of Franklin Roosevelt seemed a series of thunderclaps—shrewdly spaced, one beginning to reverberate as the sound of its predecessor died away.

FDR also had his cousin Theodore's happy faculty for orchestrating relations with the Washington correspondents, both courting and commanding them. One day, TR had seen a small group standing outside the White House gates interviewing departing visitors. He ordered an anteroom set aside for them. This became the White House Press Room. He had also developed a subtly effective press conference long before Woodrow Wilson established it formally, regularly calling in the three correspondents whose reports were most widely circulated: David Barry of the New York *Sun*'s Laffan Agency, Charles Boynton of the Associated Press, and Ed Keen of the Scripps-McRae Press Association (now United Press International). These were background-only conferences, which allowed Roosevelt a maximum range of comment and no responsibility for anything that was printed. TR was also interviewed endlessly, but he made it clear that he was not to be quoted on the disclosures that might damage him. Anyone who abused his freely given confidences was assigned to the Ananias Club and cut off from all White House news. "It was all or nothing with him," Oscar King Davis of the New York *Times* wrote later. Even those who felt the heat of TR's wrath agreed with the correspondent who wrote: "He was the master press agent of all time."

Franklin Roosevelt had learned from TR and, in quite another way, from the unfortunates whose administrations intervened. William Howard Taft, who had been a favorite of the correspondents when he served as Secretary of War—many went "Tafting" at four o'clock every afternoon, and Taft helped them dig news out of other departments—could hardly be said to have any press relations as President. Always envious of Theodore Roosevelt, he knew that he could not match that confident command. One of his aides wrote: "Neither the President nor his secretary gives out anything of real interest, nor do they understand the art of giving out news. In consequence, the papers seek their information from whatever source they can find and therefore print rumors which, if printed a month ago [during the Roosevelt Presidency] would have resulted in a clean sweep of the executive offices. Not able to find out much of the political intentions of the President or his Cabinet, they are turning their attention to the class of news known as bedroom politics. . . ."

Woodrow Wilson seemed to be reversing this policy when he announced full-fledged press conferences and called for "pitiless publicity." But when the adverse publicity came, Wilson withdrew into a shell of persecution.

Bumbling Warren G. Harding, a former newspaper publisher, tried to be a good fellow, and the correspondents protected him for a time. But he was almost totally inept. He blundered disastrously in answering one press-conference question, and Secretary of State Charles Evans Hughes pressured him into requiring that all questions be submitted in advance, in writing. This curtain separating the correspondents and the President was useful to Calvin Coolidge, a little huddle of a man whose inertia was nearly total. Hoover, like Taft, had been a favorite of the correspondents while he was a Cabinet member. But, like Wilson, he withdrew when the Depression descended, and was to the press corps a morose and sullen man.

The contrast with Franklin Roosevelt was striking. Leo Rosten has described his first press conference: "His answers were swift, positive, illuminating. He had exact information at his fingertips. He showed an impressive understanding of public problems and administrative methods. He was lavish in his confidences and background information. He was informal, communicative, gay. When he evaded a question, it was done frankly. He was thoroughly at ease." Henry M. Hyde, one of the oldest and most respected correspondents, termed it "the most amazing performance the White House has ever seen." At the end, the correspondents applauded spontaneously, for the first time in Presidential history.

What Roosevelt did in that first press conference was essentially simple: Even with a press corps of more than three hundred correspondents, he was promising the same intimate view of the Presidency that his cousin Theodore had afforded the few dozen reporters who had covered Washington a decade earlier. He said:

> I am told that what I am about to do will become impossible, but I am going to try it. We are not going to have any more

written questions; and, of course, while I cannot answer seventy-five or a hundred questions simply because I haven't got the time, I see no reason why I should not talk to you ladies and gentlemen off the record in just the way that I have been doing in Albany and in the way I used to do in the Navy Department down here. . . . There will be a great many questions, of course, that I won't answer, either because they are "if" questions—and I never answer them . . .

And the others, of course, are the questions which for various reasons I do not want to discuss, or I am not ready to discuss, or I do not know anything about. There will be a great many questions you will ask that I do not know enough about to answer.

Then, in regard to news announcements, Steve [Press Secretary Stephen Early] and I thought it would be best that straight news for use from this office should always be without direct quotation. In other words, I do not want to be directly quoted unless direct quotations are given out by Steve in writing. That makes that perfectly clear.

Then there are two other matters we will talk about: The first is "background information," which means material which can be used by all of you on your own authority and responsibility, not to be attributed to the White House, because I do not want to have to revive the Ananias Club.

Then the second thing is off-the-record information, which means, of course, confidential information which is given only to those who attend the conference. . . .

The contrast with Hoover's monosyllabic rebuffs was so stark that few correspondents seemed to catch the overtones indicating that FDR planned to be very much the master of news dissemination.

During his first term, Roosevelt was so thoroughly professional in his approach to news that Arthur Krock of the New York *Times*, seldom notably friendly to the President, declared: "He could qualify as the chief of a great copy desk." Heywood Broun called the new

Chief Executive "the best newspaperman who has ever been President of the United States."

Actually, Roosevelt's background in journalism was slender. He had been President of the *Crimson* during his student days at Harvard, then had deserted journalism for law and politics. And before his Presidency he had not been nearly so adept at disseminating news as he himself thought. As Assistant Secretary of the Navy his "Harvard arrogance" had offended a great many correspondents. As Governor of New York he was generally successful, but friction was apparent more than once, and many reporters in Albany avoided his press conferences. Clearly, Roosevelt had learned over the years.

How much he had learned was obvious in almost every meeting with the correspondents. Responding to a question about the reorganization of the NRA, he said, "Now you are getting too definite. I don't know. That is the trouble: you haven't got a spot-news story. You have an interpretative long-range story."

When he was questioned about a foreign-policy issue:

"If I were writing the story, I would put it this way: That by no stretch of the imagination has the President or the Secretary of State ever been the least bit concerned over the possibility of this oil lease involving the United States in any shape, manner or form in the Ethiopian or Italian problems. . . . And then, if I were going to write one more paragraph, I would put it this way: 'that this is another proof that since March 4, 1933, dollar diplomacy is not recognized by the American government.' "

Roosevelt was fond of instructing the correspondents in journalistic technique—and usually in a way that promoted his own point of view. He observed, when he was asked about tax stories that had appeared in several newspapers: "It is rather an interesting fact that as these stories come out of Washington, not one statement contains any reference to the very large section of our population that doesn't have a decent standard of living. . . . In other words, here's a national problem that apparently in these stories is only viewed from one angle." Then he suggested that "it would be an interesting thing for you to use your imagination on and write interpretative stories." Interpretative reporting was then a new concept, which helps explain why some anti-New Deal publishers complained that it was difficult to challenge the stories coming out of the Capital, but, somehow, Roosevelt seemed to have hypnotized the correspondents.

Eventually, however, Roosevelt's instruments of persuasion seemed to be deteriorating. He was occasionally waspish during press conferences, assigning low percentages of accuracy to columnists with national fame, labeling two reporters as dunces and inviting them to stand in the corner, paying tribute to the educational value of radio and movies and ignoring newspapers—all in public. Krock wrote that the Roosevelt Administration used "more ruthlessness, intelligence and subtlety in trying to suppress legitimate unfavorable comment than any I know."

But careful Raymond Clapper, the most respected columnist of the time, pointed out that the working press judges Presidents as men, not as archangels. If the reporters were only 60 per cent for the New Deal now, he wrote, they were still 90 per cent for the President personally. Clapper gave specific reasons for Roosevelt's continuing high standing with the press corps: Their personal contacts were usually pleasant and intimate; Roosevelt's press conferences were almost certain to yield live news; the correspondents admired the President's political skill and craftsmanship, and even when they disagreed with his purposes, they generally believed in his sincerity, courage, and readiness to experiment. Finally, the Rooseveltian theme of rescuing the forgotten man was a powerful lure for those who had investigated the real conditions of the American society.

The value of Clapper's insight became clear early in 1936. Several Republicans were jockeying for the opportunity to oppose Roosevelt in the Presidential election. Leo Rosten asked the correspondents: "Of the current candidates for President, who is your choice?" Roosevelt received fifty-four votes. His closest opponents, Governor Alfred Landon and Senator Arthur Vandenberg, received eight votes each.

Too little has been made of this, and too much of the "Fireside Chats." The President was stunningly effective over the radio—those full, confident tones that John Dos Passos called "the patroon voice, the headmaster's admonishing voice, the bedside doctor's voice that spoke to each man and to all of us." But there were few Fireside Chats: four in 1933, two in 1934, one in 1935, one in 1936. Roosevelt actually preferred to reach the people through the Washington correspondents. During the same period when he was appealing to the people over the radio exactly eight times, he held three hundred and forty press conferences. And in the 1936 election, Landon won only Maine and Vermont.

More should be made, too, of Roosevelt's shrewd use of his own expressive features. The thirties, one photographer has said, "marked the opening of a golden era for Washington cameramen. Roosevelt had a perfect sense of the dramatic and unusual." Newspaper and magazine editors clamored for any shot of that mobile and animated face. On occasion, Roosevelt punished the newspapers for opposing him by restricting pictures. In 1935, he furiously banned all pictures for a short period because a birthday photo that was snapped when he had taken off his glasses and was rubbing his eyes had been captioned, "President Ponders Farm Problem."

As a rule, only one kind of picture of the polio-crippled President was forbidden: He was never to be photographed in pain or discomfort. Once, with dozens of photographers around him, Roosevelt fell full-length on the floor. Not a picture was taken.

Otherwise, anything went. The President was shown eating hot dogs, munching peanuts at a baseball game, kissing his wife when she returned from a tour, playing with his pet Scotty, and—especially in the days immediately before he ran for a fourth term, when rumors were persistent that he was a very sick man—with his big jaw thrust forward, cigarette-holder clenched in his teeth at a jaunty angle. Looking back, it seems naïve of the anti-New Deal editorialists to have expected their readers to believe that the heavily handsome man pictured on the sands of Campobello, his mouth opened wide around a hot dog, was scheming to become a dictator.

There was much more to Roosevelt's domination of the news. At least part of the success of his Administration sprang from the work of his press secretary, Stephen Early. Unlike Herbert Hoover's inept and hesitant press men, Early was a seasoned wire-service reporter, who was given, according to another Presidential assistant, "one of the most important voices in the government." He not only worked with the President but also presided over a large and growing apparatus of public relations and information that was spread throughout the federal departments and agencies. The Roosevelt Presidency marked the firm establishment of government by publicity.

Federal press agentry had begun in a small way in 1910. Some of the members of a Congressional committee looking into the operations of the Census Bureau were startled when the director confessed that "for about six months now we have had a person whose principal duty is to act as what might properly be called, I suppose, a press agent." He was Whitman Osgood, a former reporter whose work had been thoughtfully disguised under the title "Expert Special Agent."

Soon after the discovery of this pioneer, Members of Congress themselves began to hire assistants whose principal duty was to act as what might properly be called press agents. Congressmen had always emphasized publicity, but it had been personal and somewhat erratic; Senator Pat Harrison of Mississippi was given to reminding his staff nervously, "Every day we don't get in the papers is a day lost." Congress began to fear that public-relations expertise in the Executive branch would help make the President dominant. And so in 1913 a bill was passed providing: "No money appropriated by this or any other Act shall be used for the compensation of any publicity experts unless specifically authorized for that purpose." The immediate target was President Wilson, and the proviso hampered him and his successors. But it was little more than an invitation to subterfuge during the Roosevelt era. Executive departments and agencies hired no "publicity experts"; they took on specialists in "public information" and "editing."

The fighting became intense, and a bit petty, in the mid-thirties. Senator Vandenberg proposed that Senate approval must be obtained before any Executive agency could use color printing in annual reports. Senator Harry Byrd of Virginia headed an investigating committee that turned up 270 public-information employees under the President's control. Others were hired, one correspondent wrote, even as Byrd made his report.

All in all, by putting adroit emphasis on government publicity and by catering, cajoling, and lecturing the Washington correspondents in 998 press conferences, Franklin Roosevelt orchestrated the news more artfully than any other President before him.

It was not in FDR's successor, Harry Truman, to be either artful or devious. He was so open and obvious, in fact, that even the correspondents who respected his crusty strength sometimes found it difficult to remember that they were questioning the President of the United States. As Douglass Cater has observed, the language of a reporter tends to take on the flavor of the Chief Executive he questions. The result of Truman's meetings with the Washington press corps was some of the testiest press conference prose in history.

REPORTER: Could you tell us anything about your conference with the Secretary of State and the Secretary of the Treasury?
TRUMAN: No, it's none of your business.

REPORTER: Would that mean, sir, that you would shake up the individual civilian end, service heads of the Navy Department, if this fight continues?
TRUMAN: Not necessarily. I think it will work itself out. Just wait a little.
REPORTER: I'll bet you two to one.
TRUMAN: I'll take you on that. I'll take you on that.

When the New York *Times* published a detailed story about a secret Cabinet meeting, Truman flamed about one item in the report.

TRUMAN: I never heard of it. I never *heard* of it until I saw it in the *Times*.
REPORTER: Did you know the Cabinet was meeting yesterday?

TRUMAN: Yes, the Cabinet met yesterday, but we didn't discuss that situation.

REPORTER: Where did the Cabinet meet, Mr. President? I didn't know about it.

TRUMAN: There are lots of things you don't know about. I don't have to tell you about a Cabinet meeting.

Almost everything Harry Truman said emphasized his one great quality as President: He was positive. If he had an abrasive personality, and if he sometimes seemed to suffer from an inability to think consecutively, he always gave the impression of believing devoutly in himself, in his friends, and in his program. And his hardheaded and repetitious emphasis of his beliefs made news. He spoke, as one reporter put it, "the language of Main Street, and Main Street understands it—even to the grammatical errors and slurred words." The editorials were overwhelmingly against him, but a columnist who had no great admiration for President Truman noted sagely that he had demonstrated one quality that would endear him: "He has more guts than a fiddle factory."

Critics of the press who specialize in the ghostly science of political measurements laugh at journalism by listing all the newspapers and magazines opposed to Truman in 1948, adding up their circulation figures, then capping everything with a triumphant number: Truman's two million-vote margin over Thomas E. Dewey. This seems to be convincingly common-sense evidence, but it takes account only of *editorial* opposition to the President. It ignores the fact that Truman captured the information initiative with a hurdy-gurdy, news-making campaign. As opinion analysts have long known, editorial persuasion is much more likely to be effective when the writer has the wit to make peripheral attacks rather than frontal assaults on long-held opinions. Basic beliefs can usually be eroded only subtly—by making so many exceptions to a rule that the rule itself collapses. The notion that an editorial writer can convert a Democrat to Republicanism simply by scalding "that man in the White House" is a fantasy.

While Dewey, the confident Republican nominee, was holding vaguely that "our streams must abound with fish," Truman attacked "the do-nothing Eightieth Congress." Only the most violently partisan newspapers gave their splashiest headlines to Dewey's platitudes. Most of the others, including a great many that plumped for Dewey in long-winded editorials, played up Truman's salty speeches on Page One. This is not necessarily paradoxical; some Republican publishers have an appreciation of news values that transcends their biases, and the countinghouse mentality that afflicts others told them that "our streams must abound with fish" would not sell newspapers.

Throughout the campaign of 1948, Dewey, unaware that he was running like a dry creek, seemed satisfied with his resounding victories on the editorial pages. Truman, who (like Roosevelt) has often paid tribute to working reporters in the same breath he uses to damn their publishers, preferred the news victories on the front page. The wisdom of that preference is history.

The focus on Truman the man was so relentless during his seven years as President that few noticed what was happening to the publicity apparatus he had inherited from Roosevelt. One who was alarmed by it, Congressman Christian Herter of Massachusetts, wrote: "During the recent session of Congress our federal bureaucracy revealed itself as the most powerful and potentially the most dangerous lobby of all. It fought, bureau by bureau, every Congressional move to curb its innate desire to expand. Backed by its vast, tax-supported propaganda machine . . ."

By the end of Truman's Presidency, the machine had doubled. The Executive branch had 3,632 employees working in the "Information" and "Editorial" Civil Service classifications, plus an unknown number whose titles were "Deputy Assistant Secretary for Public Affairs," "Administrative Assistant," "Executive Assistant to the Assistant Secretary," and the like. Senator Byrd, despairing of trying to decide who should stay and who should go, simply called for a general reduction of 25 per cent, hoping that a cut of that depth would result in "more news and less bull from the federal publicity mill." Characteristically, President Truman ignored him.

How astute public relations can overwhelm the Washington press corps is best revealed by the Eisenhower Presidency. And although it is doubtful that the President himself was responsible for many of the shrewd ploys, it is probably a mistake to assume that he was unknowing about publicity. After all, Eisenhower had served for decades in the U.S. Army, where the stakes are huge for one who can create a favorable image, and where the fighting for status is sometimes fierce. What often happens is revealed by the difference between an editorial written for a military newspaper that was controlled by General Douglas MacArthur and the editorial that actually appeared in it. The writer, who was apparently innocent of knowledge of the rivalry between Eisenhower and MacArthur, wrote the version that appears at the left. The version that was published after editing by officers who were more sensitive to MacArthur's wishes appears at the right:

The words of General Eisenhower Tuesday at a dinner honoring the men of Russia, Britain, and the United States who fashioned victory in Europe illustrate something fundamental about this war.

The words were spoken by a man who commanded the most powerful, the most destructive army ever put on the field by the western allies. Yet not a single line extolled the glories of war. . . .

The words of American generals, who along with their Russian and British colleagues, helped fashion victory in Europe, illustrate something fundamental about this war.

The words were spoken by men who commanded the most powerful, the most destructive armies ever put on the field in Europe. Crowds in London, in Paris, in Washington, in Chicago, in Los Angeles thronged to pay tribute to their achievements. Yet, in none. . . .

When the Eisenhower Administration took over in 1953, most of Truman's publicists were locked into place under Civil Service. Not trusting them with the Republican merchandising, Eisenhower's lieutenants added their own men. During Eisenhower's first four years, Executive information personnel nearly doubled: In 1957, the Civil Service Commission was listing 6,878 "Information and Editorial Employees." The increase continued during the second term, and Christian Herter, who had been aghast at the size of the Truman Administration's propaganda machine, eventually became Eisenhower's Secretary of State and presided unprotestingly over one of its largest units.

James Reston made the mission of this publicity complex clear in a speech before the National Conference of the Public Relations Society of America: "PR people are not doing their jobs in terms of serving the public but for the men who appoint them." Government public relations specialists, Reston charged, "have become personal press agents for their employers."

"Press agent" is too weak a word to describe the Eisenhower Administration's chief publicist, James Hagerty, just as the description of Hagerty by another correspondent—"The best Republican President who was never elected"—is too strong. But Hagerty certainly demonstrated how a canny PR man creates an image for his employer. He often made subtle decisions about which stories should involve the President. When the Atomic Energy Commission detected Russian nuclear explosions and pinpointed the location of the testing ground, the announcement clearly belonged to the AEC. But the discovery was a distinct plus. Hagerty took it over for President Eisenhower.

Similarly, the news of the first successful U.S. satellite was released not from the launching site but from Augusta, Georgia, because the President happened to be vacationing there. Later, when White House reporters asked where they could learn whether an Army satellite that had been fired that morning had gone into orbit successfully, Hagerty answered, "If it is in orbit, we will have an announcement." A correspondent who was growing wise in the ways of the press secretary then asked whether the White House would release the news if the satellite had not gone into orbit. "No," Hagerty said. The satellite did not orbit. The Army announced the failure.

Eisenhower's many vacations became widely known, but Hagerty blunted the edge of criticism by making it appear that each trip away from Washington was a working vacation. Once, when the President was golfing in Augusta, the press secretary announced the appointments of three ambassadors. The decision to appoint them had been made three weeks earlier, and the nominations were not to be sent to Congress until ten days later, but Presidential news was scarce, and Hagerty always aimed to keep Eisenhower on the front pages. It worked. Later in Augusta, Hagerty announced that Secretary of Labor James Mitchell would visit the President to discuss a bill protecting labor welfare funds. The bill had been introduced in Congress four months earlier, but the President again made the headlines.

Eventually, all the correspondents who covered the White House during the Eisenhower Presidency became aware of Hagerty's methods, but they could do little. As Russell Baker, the perceptive "Observer" columnist of the New York *Times* pointed out, "Hagerty's enduring contribution to the White House was his demonstration of how to exploit the weakness of the American newsgathering system for the promotion of his boss. . . . If editors demanded a Presidential story a day, it follows that reporters will be found to satisfy them one way or another. On days when there is no news, they will poke around darkened rooms, look under the carpet, or start staring at the west wall and adding two and two in news stories. When that sort of thing happens, the White House is in trouble. Hagerty prevented this by seeing to it that there was rarely a newsless day. If there was no news, he made a little."

When Eisenhower was recovering from coronary thrombosis in a Denver hospital, Hagerty brought in Cabinet officers and sent them to the sickroom to "confer" with the President. Then Hagerty took them to press headquarters for a news conference. The impression throughout the President's convalescence was that he had always been on top of his job. In fact, Eisenhower had been so isolated that he was not even told that the stock market had suffered its worst break since 1929 at the news of his illness.

"Because the tradition of the newspaper compels it to report with a straight face whatever is said by anyone in high office," Baker points out, "it was unable to suggest any element of charade in the parade of Cabinet officers to Denver. And so, in a sense, the press was seduced by its own morality."

The press was also seduced by its methods, especially by the time-honored "background briefing." Since background information is never attributed to the spokesman, Eisenhower's assistants soon began to use backgrounders as launching pads for trial balloons. If Congressional or public reaction to a policy announced during a backgrounder was unfavorable, the balloon was hauled down and a new policy formulated.

The celebrated "Eisenhower Doctrine" for the defense of the Middle East did not become firm policy—and was not even mentioned by the President himself*—until it had been tested in a background dinner. Actually, it had been signaled earlier with an exclusive story by James Reston. With his customary perception, Reston had put himself in the place of Secretary of State John Foster Dulles and had reasoned that defense of the troubled Middle East must at least be on the Secretary's mind. Reston confronted Dulles with this deduction, won a grudging affirmative, then published his story on December 28, 1956, quoting only "a reliable source."

This upset Dulles' timetable—he had planned to leak the doctrine later—but he tried to repair the damage by inviting a small group of correspondents to his home. There, he spelled out the doctrine: The United States was now committed to defend all of the Middle East against any encroachment by the Soviet Union.† And once again, no source could be mentioned. Columnist Roscoe Drummond's attribution was typical: "It can be stated authoritatively . . ." Reaction was favorable to the doctrine; it soon began to take on a larger and firmer shape. And, as Columnist Peter Edson

* Fairly often, Eisenhower knew little of what was going on in his Administration. He told the correspondents again and again, with weary patience, that the complete record of the pungent Dixon-Yates Contract was available—and that the record showed everyone with clean hands. Banker-businessman Adolph Wenzell, the President insisted, contrary to news reports, "was never called in or asked a single thing about the Dixon-Yates Contract." Finally, when reporters proved that the record had been doctored and that Wenzell had manipulated the contract, the President angrily bowed out with this answer to a press-conference question: "I don't intend to comment on it any more at all. . . . I don't know exactly such details as that. How can I be expected to know? I never heard of it."

† Dulles brought to full flower the meeting with the press that is half on the record, half background briefing. He announced on the record in 1958 that the United States had not decided whether to defend Quemoy against the Chinese Reds. Then he invoked the rule requiring attribution only to a "high U.S. official" and said that the Administration had definitely decided to defend Quemoy. The varying stories that came out of this conference confused everyone—including, presumably, the Chinese Reds.

dryly noted about the "Eisenhower Doctrine": "The President was playing golf in Augusta, Georgia, at the time and hadn't uttered a word on the subject."

Unfortunately for the President, not to mention the press corps, it was sometimes difficult to tell who spoke for the Administration. Eisenhower himself made this chaos possible by reacting favorably to a bit of news management by Attorney General Herbert Brownell. To encourage more support for Eisenhower, Brownell called in reporters for newspapers that had supported the President and gave them an important news break: Earl Warren had been chosen to head the Supreme Court. Raymond Brandt of the St. Louis *Post-Dispatch* angrily asked the President during his next press conference whether his Administration would continue to favor friendly newspapers. Eisenhower replied: "I think I have trusted subordinates who may occasionally leak news for purposes they consider proper."

This created a cloud of uncertainty. Who were the trusted subordinates? What purposes were proper? These questions were central to events of March, 1955, when the background briefing went wild.

The major figure was Admiral Robert Carney, Chief of Naval Operations and a militant who believed that war in Asia was imminent, inevitable, and perhaps even desirable. Ten months earlier, Admiral Carney had delivered a highly exhortatory speech comparing the fall of Dienbienphu with Munich. But this excited scant reaction. Later, the crisis in the Formosa Strait became ominous. By March, the time was right for Carney. He became the "high Administration official" featured in a background briefing. The effect was indicated by the splash it created in leading newspapers; the New York *Times* devoted three columns in the upper right-hand corner of Page One to this headline:

U.S. EXPECTS CHINESE REDS
TO ATTACK ISLES IN APRIL
WEIGHS ALL-OUT DEFENSE

This excited the response Carney wanted. War talk filled the mass media; government officials who thought the President himself had been the authority for the story began to fear war.

Unfortunately for Carney's purposes, President Eisenhower was blazing. The admiral's views, which were quite different from the President's, had been given the color of official sanction. Eisenhower could not, however, afford to fight his Navy chief in public. So, three nights after Carney's backgrounder, Hagerty held one. He repudiated the alarm—again the correspondents could cite only "a reliable source"—and on March 28 the *Times* carried another three-column headline on Page One:

EISENHOWER SEES NO WAR OVER CHINA ISLES

The effect of these contradictory reports on newspaper readers was certainly befuddlement. The effect on the papers was worse. Thanks to Hagerty, no government official had been brought into public conflict with another. All was apparent serenity within the Administration. Only the newspapers were blamed for exciting a war scare.

During much of the Eisenhower Presidency, the correspondents and the Executive establishment were battling over news sources within the establishment, usually quietly. When Brigadier General Robert Scott was accused of leaking news to promote the Air Force in its continuing rivalry with the other military services, Administration investigators revealed the subtlety of their control by playing back to him a tape recording of his own telephone calls. Secretary of Defense Robert Lovett once talked with Columnist Joseph Alsop in a Pentagon corridor because he knew that a microphone had been planted in his office.

Government control was sometimes heavy-handed. Once, when Alsop had returned to Washington after six months of reporting from Asia, two of his closest friends in government planned a reunion party. The night before it was scheduled, they called in great embarrassment to report a warning from higher up that their official positions would be compromised. The party was called off.

Alsop blazed over this and similar cases, writing: "The reporter's official acquaintances and friends are subjected to the most shameful harassment. . . . The real object is not to locate the reporter's source, but simply to strike at the reporter through the men he knows in government."

How this may have affected the correspondents is indicated by the bitter comment of one: "No investigator can work at his best when he's being investigated."

Some of the more resolute reporters proved that they were unafraid. Two years after the Eisenhower Presidency began, several correspondents were focusing hard-fact exposés on high officials. Charles Bartlett of the Chattanooga *Times* revealed that Air Secretary Harold Talbott was covertly using his Pentagon Office to promote his personnel advisory business among companies that were dependent on the Air Force for defense contracts. Then William H. Lawrence of the New York *Times* widened the investigation and gave other evidence of Talbott's quiet promotions. The impetus generated by a prestige newspaper was too strong; Talbott resigned.

Other correspondents were responsible for the resignations of Richard Mack, a member of the Federal Communications Commission, who accepted money from an interested party in the award of a Miami television license; Robert Tripp Ross, an Assistant Secretary of Defense whose wife and brother-in-law were shown to be benefiting from multi-million-dollar uniform contracts with the Army; and John C. Doerfer of the Federal Communications Commission. David Wise of the New York *Herald Tribune* reported that Doerfer had taken a six-day Atlantic cruise on a yacht owned by a Miami Beach broadcasting company president. Doerfer tried to weather the storm blown up by Wise's report, vowing that he would continue as a member of the FCC. Then all three Washington newspapers attacked him editorially. Doerfer resigned.

The most sensational and far-reaching exposé came in 1958, when months of investigation by several correspondents resulted in news stories that revealed the easy morality of Sherman Adams,

Assistant to the President and, next to Eisenhower, the most power-ful figure in government. The New York *Post* was the first to report that Adams had accepted gifts from Bernard Goldfine. Others broad-ened and deepened the investigation, eventually showing that Adams had used his office to help Goldfine. The pressure from publications that had supported the Administration became so intense that not even a public appeal from Eisenhower himself ("But I need him") could save Adams.

And yet, any balanced assessment of the Eisenhower years shows that the Administration won its battle with the correspondents. Only the exposure of Adams aroused public furor, and only the exposure of Adams blemished Eisenhower's prestige.

Counter-publicity muffled each of the other exposures of Eisen-hower Administration officials. Hagerty was especially adept at re-leasing big, positive stories to compete with the headlines of exposé. And then Eisenhower himself had a certain talent for divorcing him-self from the mistakes of his own Administration. This is best re-vealed by the curious case of Wolf Ladejinsky, an official with twenty years of distinguished service, who had been ousted as a security risk by the Department of Agriculture. Largely as a result of agitation by Correspondent Clark Mollenhoff, who sometimes seems to be making a career of altering government decisions, Ladejinsky was reinstated. But during one fantastic period, even as Secretary of Agriculture Ezra Taft Benson was persuading President Eisenhower that Ladejinsky was potentially a bad risk ("That would scare me," the President told Benson after looking at the Agriculture Depart-ment's file on Ladejinsky), Eisenhower was approving the hiring of Ladejinsky by Harold Stassen, Director of the Foreign Operations Administration.

The President revealed how neatly he washed his hands of such muddy affairs during his press conference of January 12, 1955. Ben-son's firing Ladejinsky as too great a risk for the Department of Agriculture and Stassen's hiring him as a qualified executive for the Foreign Operations Administration was, the President decided, "a nice balance in the case." When a perplexed correspondent wanted to know how Ladejinsky could both be a security risk and not be

one, Eisenhower replied that human judgments are certain to differ
and that Ladejinsky's loyalty was now Stassen's problem: "If something should turn up to show that his judgment was wrong, then he
was the one to be held responsible." In short, the President does not
really have the ultimate responsibility for his Administration; a lesser
official must take the blame.

How this worked to Eisenhower's advantage in periods of extreme stress is revealed by the U-2 incident—the ill-fated flight over
Russia in 1960 of an American reconnaissance plane piloted by
Francis Gary Powers. Khrushchev announced on May 5 that the
plane had been shot down, but he said nothing at the time about the
fate of the pilot.

Speaking for the Eisenhower Administration, the National Aer-
onautics and Space Administration claimed that the plane had wandered during a flight designed to collect weather information. NASA
issued an elaborate account of scientific study through high-altitude
weather observation. Khrushchev's charge that the plane was on an
espionage mission was made to seem a crude bluster.

Assuming that the pilot had been killed, much of the American
press devoted the next two days to predictable editorials like this one
published in the New York *Mirror:*

THE WORD IS "MURDER"

Premier Khrushchev personally ordered the rocket-destruc-
tion of an unarmed U.S. aircraft which had drifted into Soviet
air space, probably because its pilot became unconscious when
his oxygen equipment failed. . . . Khrushchev has revealed
himself and his beastly character to the full; he is a pig in human
form.

Then, as American indignation heightened, Khrushchev sprang
his trap: the plane had been downed 1,300 miles into Soviet territory,
not just across the border. Moreover, Pilot Powers was alive and had
confessed that he had been sent aloft by the Central Intelligence
Agency to photograph Russian military installations.

The U.S. government recovered from this shock by stages. First, the Department of State admitted that the plane had "probably" been on an intelligence mission and that the original explanation for the flight "had not been entirely accurate." Ultimately, government spokesmen reached the point of defending the spy mission. Significantly, however, the State Department denied that the flight had been authorized by "officials in Washington," thus protecting President Eisenhower.

Meanwhile, the press was recovering gradually. At first, columnists and editorial writers posed serious questions about what the New York *Herald Tribune* called "the equivocal position in which our government has been placed." Then Khrushchev loosed a flood of invective at the United States and its President, and the querying tone of the press changed abruptly. Most newspapers began to echo the demand of the New York *Journal-American* that U.S. citizens "form up" behind their government. Form up they did, in a flood of chauvinistic editorials and letters to the editor. Spying and lying were defended on the ground of necessity. For many, the U-2 incident became a point of pride—proof that the United States would fight the Communist world with its own weapons.

Not until this point was reached did Mr. Eisenhower emerge to speak for his Administration. The ultimate responsibility, he said, rested with the President, and he would gladly assume it. He was cheered for his forthrightness.

CHAPTER EIGHT

The News Managers—II

HENRY BRANDON of the London *Sunday Times:* Do you think the President's indefatigable interest in the press was an advantage or a disadvantage to him?

ARTHUR SCHLESINGER, Jr., Special Assistant to President Kennedy: Oh, I think it was over-all an advantage. One of the important things the President has to do is to know what's going on. . . . Some, like Coolidge and Eisenhower, just didn't read papers which criticized them; others, like Roosevelt, Kennedy, Johnson, and Truman, read them with apparently inexhaustible capacity for indignation.

"A reporter suggested to an LBJ aide that the President looked a bit tired. 'Look, I wouldn't write that,' the uneasy aide said. 'If he reads it, he'll double his schedule and go twice as hard to prove you wrong.' "

—Correspondent PETER LISAGOR

REPORTER: "Mr. President, is expansion of the Vietnam war into Laos or North Vietnam a live possibility at this point?"

PRESIDENT JOHNSON: "I don't want to give you any particular guideposts as to your conduct in the matter, but when you crawl out on a limb, you always have to find another to crawl back on.

"And I have just been sitting here in the serene atmosphere of the Pedernales for the last few days reading about the wars that you have involved us in, and the additional undertakings that I have made decisions on, or that General Taylor has recommended, or that Mr. McNamara plans, or that Secretary Rusk envisages.

"In retrospect, as you look back over all of your writings, they are somewhat similar as they are today. I don't know whether you have a black sheet that you take out and, every time we have a meeting on it, rewrite it."

IN the spring of 1963, a newspaper publisher who had just received the latest Gallup Poll showing the country's attitudes toward its President swore bitterly: "I just can't understand it. We've *exposed* Kennedy. We've shown that he's been failing and lying to the American people. . . . And yet they're making a god of him!"

It was an understandable reaction, and not only because the publisher had been a whole-souled supporter of Richard Nixon.

President Kennedy had just experienced the winter of his deepest discontent. His administration was failing the task it had set for itself in Laos and Vietnam. It had failed to get the country moving while adding hugely to the national debt. Perhaps most important, government officials had admitted that, to put it gently, they had told less than the truth about the Cuban crisis of October, 1962. The whole orchestra had fallen downstairs at once; the critics were in full cry. And yet less than one fourth of the American people— exactly 24 per cent—disapproved of the way John F. Kennedy was performing as President.

A full view of the facts deepens the paradox, especially if one looks at the Administration's heavy-handed guides to reporting the Cold War. Secretary of Defense Robert McNamara set the tone shortly after he began his rule at the Pentagon. He had a plaintive question for correspondents who were revealing flaws in American weaponry: "Why should we tell Russia that the Zeus developments may not be satisfactory? What we ought to be saying is that we have the most perfect anti-ICBM system that the human mind can devise." The fact that McNamara was simply arguing for false reports became clear when, shortly after he had suggested that correspondents describe the Nike-Zeus program glowingly, he scrapped it.

Then came the abortive Bay of Pigs invasion in 1961, only three months after Kennedy's Inauguration. Reporters were told at the height of the invasion that 5,000 patriotic refugees were penetrating Cuba. In fact, a force of 1,400 was involved. Like McNamara's guideline on Nike-Zeus, this was designed to mislead the enemy by misleading everybody.

In August, 1962, Senator Kenneth Keating of New York made his sensational charge that Russia was arming Cuba. In October, he said that the Russians were building intermediate-range ballistic-missile sites for Castro. But White House, State Department, and Defense Department officials held that there was nothing to Senator Keating's charges. Only when the build-up in Cuba had gone so far that President Kennedy announced a quarantine of Cuba and issued an ultimatum to Russia did the Administration admit that Keating had been right all along.

The chief justification for lying was supplied by Arthur Sylvester, a former correspondent who had become Assistant Secretary of Defense for Public Affairs. While covering Washington for the Newark *News*, Sylvester had been fond of proclaiming: "The only way for a newspaperman to look at a bureaucrat is *down!*" Having become a bureaucrat, Sylvester was apparently concerned that the correspondents might look down at him. And so he overexplained, beginning with: "In the kind of world we live in, the generation of news by actions taken by the government becomes one weapon in a strained situation. The results justify the methods we used." Later, still at pains to justify himself, Sylvester declared at a meeting of Sigma Delta Chi, the professional journalism fraternity: "I think the inherent right of the government to lie—to lie to save itself when faced with nuclear disaster—is basic, *basic*."

This is the kind of home truth that no government official is ever supposed to admit. Six months later, such a storm had blown up over it that, as Sylvester headed for a hearing to explain himself again, this time to Congress, another Administration official advised: "Never, under any circumstances whatever, use the word lie. Don't use it negatively; don't use it positively. If you have to tell the committee you want to lie down, say recline."

Congress and the correspondents exerted intense pressure, but instead of easing the flow of information, the Administration clamped on even tighter restrictions. Defense officials were not allowed to talk to correspondents unless a third person was present or unless the officials submitted written reports on their interviews. Robert Manning, Sylvester's counterpart in the State Department, adopted a similar policy, explaining that it was about time he got an idea how many State Department people were helping him with his job of dispensing information. When correspondents protested, Manning maintained that the Department was still as "wide open as Yankee Stadium"—to which a reporter responded, "Yes, but we have trouble with the turnstiles." Odd subterfuges developed. Certain that offices were bugged with hidden microphones (as in the Eisenhower Administration), correspondents began to interview their favorite Pentagon and State Department officials by talking to them quietly while on ostensibly casual strolls through the corridors.

It was a strained period; the Administration seemed to be at swords' points with the press corps. The time seemed right for a Congress eager to re-establish Congressional government. The Executive and Legislative branches met in the most meaningful clash of the Kennedy Era: Senator John McClellan brought the full force of his fearsome investigations subcommittee to bear on the award of a TFX plane contract to General Dynamics. It was a case rich in sensational details. Costs would run into billions. It was made to order for McClellan. But after nine months of investigation and widely publicized hearings, it was obvious that the Senator had failed. One of his associates said in a baffled tone: "But when John investigates them, they're supposed to *stay* investigated."

The Administration did not stay investigated for one reason: Every Congressional publicity thrust was countered. The correspondents who were deemed eager to attack the Administration instead co-operated when Defense officials leaked information and held background briefings. Congress was not only held to be wrong but was accused of "Gestapo tactics" and of pursuing the case for less than altruistic motives. Clark Mollenhoff, on the side of Congress, as usual, was embittered by the refusal of his colleagues to take up the Congressional case. In the end, it was labeled "the TFX Inquiry" —not, significantly, "the TFX Scandal." On such labels does public opinion turn. Congress was made to seem an antique and fusty subgovernment, frustrating a strong Chief Executive.

Hence, the bewilderment of the anti-Kennedy publisher. And hence the need for explaining John Kennedy's continuing appeal.

News management, and mismanagement, did not mar the Kennedy image for a simple reason: He was the most sophisticated shaper of public opinion in Presidential history.

Kennedy's information policies were complicated—and sometimes contradictory—but their thrust was not to be found in the blunders of the beleaguered Defense Department. The center of information was the White House, and there the policy was the precise reverse of censorship. Never before had Washington correspondents been given so full a view of the President and the Presidency—which is to say they were invited to feel with Kennedy the crushing responsibility, and to be enveloped in the aura, of the greatest center of leadership in the Western world.

The value of this policy springs from the fact that a stark view of the Presidency is overwhelming. Talking to a President who has charm and toughness and keen intelligence, few Americans will fail to admire him. More than anything else, the open White House enabled Kennedy—who had the awesome responsibility of deciding when or whether the world would end—to become the dominant source of news, explanation, and opinion.

Only one who worked as a Washington correspondent during both the Eisenhower and Kennedy administrations can appreciate how profoundly John Kennedy revolutionized the reporting of the Presidency. The single innovation of the Eisenhower Presidency was the televised press conference, and Eisenhower required that his conferences be filmed so they could be edited before release. In contrast, live television coverage of Kennedy's conferences was only one of many innovations.

Before 1961, the White House had been largely a closed preserve. Information was usually channeled through the President's press secretary, and some White House correspondents never so much as met some of the President's chief assistants. The almost invariable reply of Eisenhower assistants who were asked for interviews was "See Hagerty." One correspondent who arranged an interview with a Presidential speechwriter without going through the press secretary was so elated that he telephoned his editor to say, "I broke around behind Hagerty!" The important news was not the substance of the interview but the fact that he got one.

When Kennedy took over in 1961, correspondents wandered through the White House offices in such numbers that they created a traffic problem.

President Kennedy's staff did much to influence favorable press coverage, but the President was his own most effective promoter. He practiced personal salesmanship with the *élan* of one accustomed to establishing the rules of the game. Franklin Roosevelt granted one exclusive interview, to Arthur Krock of the New York *Times*. Harry Truman granted one, also to Krock. In both cases, the storm of protest blowing up among other correspondents was so violent that neither ever tried again. (Anne O'Hare McCormick of the *Times* spoke to Roosevelt privately and obtained authoritative views, but she produced nothing properly describable as an interview story. Krock has written that Truman granted one other exclusive interview but required that the source be veiled.) Eisenhower observed the protocol. But Kennedy, from the beginning, made such a fetish of giving exclusive interviews that his press secretary, Pierre Salinger, once observed that he often had to go to the President's office to get to see the White House correspondents.

Kennedy, James Reston wrote, broke every rule in the book:

When he came into the White House, he was warned by his newspaper friends about all the wicked ways of the press, particularly their jealousy and their hostility toward anyone who gives special advantages to any individual reporter.

The President indicated how seriously he took this warning at the very beginning of his Administration. After his Inaugural Ball, he suddenly showed up at Joseph Alsop's house. . . .

A few days later he drove around to Walter Lippmann's house for a talk, went to dinner at the home of Rowland Evans of the New York *Herald Tribune* and later had his old friend Charles Bartlett of the Chattanooga *Times* up to Hyannis Port for the weekend.

When some of the President's associates asked the President whether this was wise, he took the original view that reporters were also members of the Human Race, and added that he proposed to see anybody he liked and even some reporters he didn't like.

Reston warned his fellow correspondents of the lure of the new order with: "It is hard to go into that House that means so much to us historically and not be impressed with it and with the terrible burdens the President has to carry. How could you help but be sympathetic? Once you become sympathetic it becomes increasingly difficult to employ the critical faculties." Yet Reston himself, who was once proud that he had never talked alone with a President during twenty years in Washington—having feared, he explained, that he might get "tied up"—yielded often to the lure of exclusive Presidential interviews.

It is doubtful that Reston, an exceedingly tough-minded man, got tied up for long. But the general effect of Presidential attention is shown by the actions of another leading correspondent who got a call from the White House saying that the President wanted to see him. It was a snowy day. With a show of nonchalance, the correspondent drew on one of his galoshes and went clumping out the door toward the elevator, leaving the other on his desk.

Surely the effect of the scores of private interviews Mr. Kennedy granted were favorable to him. The most astonishing coup came when, shortly before the death of Columnist George Sokolsky, President Kennedy won over that high priest of conservatism. Later, when Walter Lippmann was critical of the Administration's policy on Berlin, the President drove over to Lippmann's home and outlined his problems. Lippmann promptly wrote a sympathetic column picturing the cross-pressures at work on the President. And when the corps of young foreign correspondents led by David Halberstam began to report the harsh facts about the failure in Vietnam—facts quite different from the Administration line—Kennedy's friend Joseph Alsop flew to the scene and wrote a shrill column that was only a tone below charging the foreign correspondents with subversion.

From the beginning, Mr. Kennedy was amazingly accessible. He invited correspondents to his parties and attended theirs, and once wryly summarized his own sociability with: "It's hard not to get invited to the White House these days." He was quick to congratulate first-rate writers, and even anti-Kennedy columnists like Holmes Alexander and William S. White were thrown off balance by words of praise and warm notes. Kennedy captured one correspondent who had been critical of his speaking techniques by opening their interview with: "You're right. I can't read a speech worth a damn."

The resulting praise for the President was predictable, but it came in such a flood during the early months that one Kennedy admirer and biographer, James MacGregor Burns, commented acidly:

> . . . He is not only the handsomest, the best dressed, the most articulate, and graceful as a gazelle. He is omniscient; he swallows and digests whole books in minutes; his eye seizes instantly on the crucial point of a long memorandum; he confounds experts with superior knowledge of their field. He is omnipresent; no sleepy staff member can be sure that he will not telephone—or pop in; every hostess at a party can hope that he will. He is omnipotent; he personally bosses and spurs the whole shop; he has no need of Ike's staff apparatus; he is more than a lion, more than a fox. He's Superman!

Burns' own admiration for the President was realistic, and he feared that when the pendulum swung back the other way, criticism of Kennedy would be vicious—a kind of balance for the adulation that had been poured out at the beginning. Inevitably, the pendulum did swing. During periods of crisis, some pundits defined Kennedy's pragmatism as an encounter of the unprepared with the unforeseen. The President ruefully confessed at one point that he had been "reading more and enjoying it less." But the force of criticism was blunted by the President himself. During a press conference shortly after the Cuban Crisis of 1962, he made concessions to the press corps, announcing that the restrictions imposed on interviews with officials of the State and Defense Departments would be modified. But he also challenged the correspondents, asking whether their complaints amounted to a suggestion that "any member of the Defense Department should speak on any subject to any newspaperman and the newspaperman should print it or not print it as he sees fit?"

The amalgam of conciliation and challenge in that press conference epitomized Kennedy's relations with the correspondents. He was at once their warm friend and severest critic. On at least a dozen occasions, he called down correspondents in person. Merriman Smith of UPI echoed the general amazement at the wide-ranging reading of all the Kennedys with: "How they can spot an obscure paragraph in a paper of 3,000 circulation 2,000 miles away is beyond me. They must have a thousand little gnomes reading the papers for them."

The President's bluntness caused some antagonism, but the side effects were positive. Reporters who had been tempted during the Eisenhower Era to do half their work because they were writing of a President who read little had to check every fact when Kennedy took over; a President who reads at a rate of 1,200 words a minute might read *their* stories. In addition, of course, Presidential criticism of the correspondents tended to quell correspondents' criticism of the President; only the toughest reporter is insensitive to the ire of a President.

But the most important effect was paradoxical. Kennedy's very criticisms were, in effect, complimentary, making it apparent that political journalism mattered. It was an implicit recognition of the crucial role of the Washington correspondent.

The real importance to the Kennedy Administration of one correspondent, John Scali of the American Broadcasting Company, did not become generally known for nearly two years. At the beginning of the Cuban missile crisis of October, 1962, Scali, who had long been a respected diplomatic correspondent, received an urgent call from an official of the Russian Embassy in Washington. The Russian, Alexander Fomin, suggested a settlement of the crisis and urged that Scali put it before the State Department. The proposal was that missile bases be dismantled under U.N. supervision in exchange for a United States pledge not to invade Cuba. For three tense days, Scali, in effect was the chief U.S. spokesman. When Khrushchev demanded the following day that American missile bases in Turkey be abandoned in return for Russian dismantling of the Cuban bases, Scali met Fomin in a deserted hotel ballroom and, pounding on a chair, called the new proposal "a dirty, rotten, lousy, stinking double cross." The new demand, Scali told the Russian, was totally unacceptable. It worked. Russia backed away.

Hoping that Scali could retain his relationship with Fomin, and fearing that releasing the details might seem a deliberate affront to

Khrushchev, Kennedy asked Scali to say nothing of his role. Instead, the President offered to write a personal letter of thanks. Eager to write the most significant story of his career, Scali rejoined that the letter would do him about as much good as it would do the President to be "renominated by the Democratic National Convention in secret." The President threw up his hands and laughed, then asked that the story be withheld until he left the White House. After Kennedy's death, Scali won the permission of the State Department to break the story. Ironically, Robert Donovan of the Los Angeles *Times* learned of it and broke it first.

Kennedy's sense of the importance of journalism did not come to him in any quick flash of insight. It flowed from his sense of history and was developed long before he became President. Traces are apparent in *Profiles in Courage*, which was written in 1955. The theme begins with four quotations; one by Ernest Hemingway, one by a former Cabinet member—and two by syndicated columnists. The press and its influence are threaded through to the end of the book. In one of the most revealing passages, Senator Kennedy wrote that the politically courageous today must face the fact that "our every-day life is becoming so saturated with the tremendous power of mass communications that any unpopular or unorthodox course arouses a storm of protests such as John Quincy Adams—under attack in 1807 —could never have envisioned."

Not long after writing these words, Kennedy emphasized his understanding of the power of the press in a speech on the floor of the Senate. He was engaged in a heated debate with Price Daniel of Texas, arguing the merits of a proposal to change the Electoral College system of electing the American President. As evidence of the need for change, Senator Daniel cited the disputed election of Rutherford B. Hayes, who ran against Samuel Tilden in 1876: "The fraud which is continually referred to in the Hayes-Tilden case was a fraud that grew up under the present electoral system which is being followed today."

Senator Kennedy responded quickly: "Oh, no, the fraud was discovered as the result of the New York *Times*' refusal to accept the election of Tilden. On the night of the election, the *Times* sent telegrams to the various states to make sure they held the line for Hayes; thus it was the result of Senator Lamar and other influential members of the electoral commission making a deal that Hayes would withdraw Federal troops from the South that they agreed to the election of Hayes. Had it not been for four journalists, sitting up that night in the New York *Times* office, the election of Tilden would have been the official result. But these four men changed the course of history." (Ironically, in this most incisive performance of his career in Congress, Senator Kennedy helped to preserve the Electoral College in its historic form and thus assured his own election a few years later. The adoption of the Presidential election formula prescribed in Senator Daniel's Senate Joint Resolution 31 would have resulted in Kennedy's defeat in 1960.)

Kennedy's sharp sense of the power of journalism became especially valuable during his Presidential campaign. Most candidates make up to the press, but affection and respect cannot be faked successfully. Kennedy had himself worked as a political reporter, and his liking for journalists who developed sharp insights in flavorful phrases was obviously genuine. This was matched by his assistants. Theodore White has written that they "gave off a sense of joy when they greeted a correspondent joining or rejoining the circuit, as if they had waited for him, and him alone, to arrive—and then whispered to him a little nugget of color or some anecdote that his particular magazine or newspaper would want."

This was in stark contrast to the dank air that enveloped the correspondents traveling with Nixon. *His* assistants chose to make coverage difficult. "*Stuff* the bastards!" one Nixon aide exploded. "They're all against Dick anyway." As the campaign progressed, some of the correspondents who followed Kennedy became his friends, many were his devoted admirers, and nearly all diverted themselves by singing cutting songs about Nixon and the Republicans as the Kennedy entourage made its way across the nation. On the Nixon side, the correspondents composed malicious parodies of his speeches for their own private amusement: "GUTHRIE CENTER, IOWA

—Vice President Nixon said today farmers should eat their way out of the surplus problem."

The abrasive edge of Nixon's relationships with the correspondents symbolized the worst mistake of the Republican campaign. Nixon had proved before—notably during intensive interviews by Earl Mazo of the New York *Herald Tribune* and Stewart Alsop of the *Saturday Evening Post*—that he could present himself winningly to the searching examination of correspondents who were inclined to dislike him. Moreover, the reporting of a Presidential campaign is not limited to fashioning news stories from speech notes. It calls for fleshing out a man, highlighting the color and flavor of a personality who is in quest of the nation's highest office—and this is a practice that works to the advantage of *any* personable candidate. By avoiding the correspondents, Nixon made their work impossible and negated a source of his own strength.

(Almost incredibly, Goldwater, who is so personable that he had more to gain from relaxed association with the correspondents, repeated Nixon's mistake. Although the correspondents were overwhelmingly for Johnson, they had also been strong for Stevenson in 1952 and 1956, which did not prevent Eisenhower from winning votes by making himself available for "human stories." As the uncompromisingly liberal T.R.B. of *The New Republic* pointed out: "Many of our newspaper colleagues have liked Barry as a person more than Lyndon. They would have preferred him as a next-door neighbor." It was especially important that the correspondents get close to Goldwater during the campaign. Distance from a candidate whose every statement must be interpreted breeds confusion. When one of Goldwater's assistants complained in some desperation, "Don't write what he *says*, write what he *means*," one reporter retorted, "How can I tell?")

Had Richard Nixon become President and died as Kennedy died, it may be that the mass media would have reacted as they did during the days that followed November 22, 1963. Certainly, page after page in newspapers and magazines and day after day on radio and television would have been devoted to his life, his work, and his memory. And yet it is difficult to imagine the same spirit, the same deep sense of shock and loss. This is not alone because Kennedy captured most of the Washington correspondents; he also captured with his grace and style much of the mass media—Republican in ownership and sentiment though the majority of them were and are.

The boldest and most successful instrument of Kennedy's press policy was known somewhat cynically around the White House as "Operation Publisher." It began before the Inauguration, when Kennedy invited North Carolina publishers to dinner and talked to them about his problems and policies. Then he began bringing publishers from all over the nation to the White House for confidential two-hour luncheons.

"Operation Publisher" was extraordinarily useful. How adroitly the President used the meetings was made clear by a Republican publisher's description of the luncheon he attended: "Everything is handled in such an informal manner you feel at ease. The President asked us for our opinions on a number of matters. He told us that he liked to have as much background as possible before making a decision. The President speaks so frankly about things that you get a feeling that he trusts you and is taking you into his confidence."

Not all the publishers felt as flattered or became as friendly, but the educational effect of sharing the world's problems with critics is revealed in the statement of another Republican: "I came to Washington quite critical of foreign aid. I had the feeling that the money was not getting to the people who need it and we were not doing enough to insist that other well-to-do countries bear their share. I spoke to the President about this. He gave me some good answers. I must say that he convinced me that we are doing right. I told him that I just wished that all 180 million Americans could have heard his answer."

The only law requiring that Presidents hold press conferences, Arthur Krock once observed, is the political law of self-preservation. Nothing better illustrates the point—or makes it more obvious that Presidents use the mass media for their own ends—than the stark difference between the press conferences of John Kennedy and Lyndon Johnson.

Kennedy was slender, handsome, magnetic, and the possessor of a quick mind and an articulate tongue. He was ideally equipped for the mass conferences staged in the State Department auditorium —an auditorium so large that, to give the impression of a packed house, the television cameras were placed not at the rear but at the halfway point, with the correspondents crowded in between the cameras and the President. In the words of one correspondent, "Kennedy glittered—he positively glittered—up on that platform. No wonder he wanted live television!"

Johnson, whose widely known ego is not quite as inflated as his political acumen, knew better than to match himself immediately against the memory of Kennedy's performances. Johnson is attractive in person, but he is also earthy in a typically Texas way, with more than a strain of vulgarity. In the company of sophisticates, he sometimes becomes aware of his cattle-and-tumbleweed manner. He once asked a friend, "When are you going to help me wipe this tobacco stain off my jaw?"

The kind of press conference Johnson prefers was apparent from the first. Two weeks after he became President, twenty-five of the regular White House correspondents went to the office of Press Secretary Pierre Salinger for what had been announced as a routine briefing. Suddenly, they found themselves ushered into the President's office. It was a highly informal conference. Navy mess attendants served coffee; the President sat in a cushioned rocking chair at the head of two semicircular couches; the correspondents sat on the couches, sipping coffee and asking occasional questions to further the rambling flow of Johnson's conversation.

Ten days later, Johnson held another surprise press conference that was almost as informal as the first. Then, during an extended work-vacation at the LBJ Ranch in Texas, he held no fewer than four impromptu conferences, one of them beside a haystack, another at a party given by the correspondents. He became wildly experimental. There was a conference in the old White House theater; another in the spacious East Room; another on the south lawn. The conferences became mobile: seven laps around the White House grounds. They became expansive: the reporters' wives and children were invited. Finally, the Baltimore *Sun* asked somewhat plaintively, "Will the next press conference be tonight, tomorrow or next week? Will it be held on horseback? In the White House swimming pool? Will the public be invited and the press excluded?"

The great value for Mr. Johnson of his spur-of-the-moment press conferences is that he faces only the White House correspondents, avoiding questions from the specialists who cover the rest of Washington—specialists who do not have a vested interest in remaining on good terms with the President. Another is that the intimate atmosphere of small conferences discourages embarrassing questions. The Bobby Baker case was at the height of interest during Johnson's first weeks as President, yet he was asked nothing about it during his first two meetings with the press. Perhaps the chief value for the President is that he can control an informal conference. Instead of submitting himself to a half hour of questioning in the Kennedy-type conference, which is controlled by the correspondents, the President can start and end as he likes. The importance of this factor became evident one Saturday two months after Johnson took office, when a rumor ran through the press corps that another impromptu conference was likely. By two thirty that afternoon, more than a hundred reporters were milling about. The President waited until five to call them in. He alluded to the fact that he had heard complaints about "quickie conferences," and invited questions with what sounded like a warning: "I never enjoy anything more than polite, courteous, fair, judicious reporters, and I think all of you qualify." Then, after responding to a tentative question, he swerved into the Bobby Baker case and explained that his own involvement was innocent. Before the correspondents could pin down his exact relationship to Baker's deals, the President turned and walked out.

Not until his hundredth day in office did he schedule a traditional mass conference, after which James Reston commented: "President Johnson achieved his major objective in his first live televised press conference: He survived."

It is not surprising that Johnson favors intimate, face-to-face meetings. He is seldom effective when his questioners are distant and questions are pointed. During one "Meet the Press" program in 1960 he responded to questions throughout the half-hour program and answered not one directly. (Lawrence Spivak has said that he barely restrained himself from asking later, "Now that we're off the air, will you tell us if your name is Lyndon Johnson?") Up close, Johnson is overpowering. Ted Lewis of the New York *Daily News* has pointed out: "Johnson is formidably ingratiating—in private or semi-private gatherings. He easily dominates any group where he can look a man in the eye, grab lapels, poke chests, and talk about what happens to be on his mind."

How this affects correspondents who talk to Johnson alone was revealed by Stewart Alsop of the *Saturday Evening Post*. While Johnson was Senate Majority Leader, Alsop wrote an article suggesting that Democrats as well as Republicans were vulnerable on the defense issue. The article contained these two fatal sentences: "As for Johnson, his voting record on defense has been good. But he is obviously open to the charge that he only summoned his Preparedness Subcommittee to make a serious inquiry into preparedness after the issue had been dramatized by the Sputniks."

Alsop later wrote:

. . . On the day the article appeared, the reporter was summoned to the majority leader's small, ornate, oddly impressive office in the Capitol. Treatment A started quietly. The majority leader was, it seemed, in a relaxed, friendly, and reminiscent mood. Nostalgically he recalled how he had come to Washington in 1937, a mere freshman Congressman, and how Franklin D. Roosevelt had prevailed on the chairman of the Naval Affairs Committee to put "young Lyndon Johnson" on his powerful committee. That was, it seemed, the beginning of Johnson's interest in the national defense, which had continued ever since.

By gradual stages the relaxed, friendly and reminiscent mood gave way to something rather like a human hurricane. Johnson was up, striding about his office, talking without pause, occasionally leaning over, his nose almost touching the mesmerized reporter's, to shake the reporter's shoulder or grab his knee. Secretaries were rung for. Memoranda appeared and then more memoranda, as well as letters, newspaper articles and unidentifiable scraps of paper, which were proffered in quick succession and then snatched away. Appeals were made, to the Almighty, to the shades of the departed great, to the reporter's finer instincts and better nature, while the reporter, unable to get a word in edgewise, sat collapsed upon a leather sofa, eyes glazed, mouth half open. Treatment A ended a full two hours later, when the majority leader, a friendly arm around the shoulder of the dazed journalist, ushered him into the outer office. It was not until some days later that the reporter was able to recall that, excellent as Johnson's record on national defense undoubtedly is, the two sentences he had written had been demonstrably true.

A healthy respect for Treatment A helps explain why, as Alsop noted, Johnson's friends and admirers among the correspondents tend to write "what Lyndon Johnson wants them to write." But there are varying other reasons why two of the toughest minds in the Washington press corps sometimes write as though they were on Johnson's staff. One of Drew Pearson's staunchest supporters, a correspondent who had long defended the columnist's inaccuracies with: "Pearson uses half-truths to smoke out the whole truth," now calls him "Lyndon's lackey." William S. White, who is at times a valuable spokesman for moderate conservatism, need not have bothered to inform his readers that he and Johnson are close friends. Nearly everything he writes makes that clear. Johnson was hardly in office before White was publishing *The Professional*, which is surely the most embarrassingly appreciative political biography ever written.

Nonetheless, and contrary to the deep belief of some Republicans, some correspondents have been pointing up Johnson's flaws from the beginning—his massive ego, his cornball sentiments, his occasional inclination to treat the truth casually. Few political reporters can be entirely drawn to a man who flies a personal flag and stamps his initials on everything he touches. Several pointed out the flapdoodle in Johnson's proposal that Washington build "a memorial to God." Some noted the paradox of his saving pennies on the White House electric bill and planning to spend thousands to equip a Presidential television studio. A great many pointed to the falsity of Johnson's melodramatic announcement in 1964, not long before the campaigns began, that a railroad strike had been averted. The President considered the settlement such a coup that he would not wait for television to come to him. He drove out to the CBS studio in Washington to go on the air as soon as possible. In concluding the announcement, he read a letter from Cathy May Baker of Park Forest, Illinois, who had appealed to the President to stop the strike so her grandmother could travel to Park Forest from Yonkers, New York, for Cathy's first communion. Johnson's whole-souled happiness that Cathy's grandmother would now be able to make the trip no doubt won him more than his share of the grandmother vote. The trouble was that the letter had been written two weeks earlier, and Cathy had experienced her first communion, with grandmother on hand, the Saturday before.

Mr. Johnson's inability to distinguish the moving from the maudlin is a wounding flaw, but if he eventually suffers the worst press relations of any President since Hoover, the reason is likely to be quite different. He is a devious man who seems determined to enhance his reputation as an operator. This would be bad enough if only the correspondents were aware of it. Significantly, though, a United Press International executive returned from a trip to Kansas early in 1965 and reported that no one was asking about the President's policies and program; the concern was with what he was trying to hide. Was his cold worse than we were led to believe? Why is he reluctant to hold big news conferences as Kennedy did? Many questions emphasized "real" and "really": What is our *real* position in Vietnam?

The pressure on the correspondents to try to get at the truth is unusually intense because a great many readers have become skeptical about the news from Washington. "Do you think the newspapers are dishonest?" the troubled UPI executive asked a history professor who had expressed doubt that the *real* facts are available. "No," he responded, "but don't you people get taken in by government officials?" The UPI executive answered that he thought the Washington correspondents were sophisticated enough to prevail in the end over attempts to manage the news.

This is undoubtedly right, but the very fact that the press corps must work to "prevail in the end" emphasizes the difficulty of getting the truth at the beginning. The jousting with Mr. Johnson is different from that with Mr. Kennedy, whose secrets related almost entirely to Cold-War strategy. President Johnson is almost pathologically eager to cloak the facts about Southeast Asia—the use of nausea gas in Vietnam was so well hidden that it took the press nearly two months to dig it out—but he is equally concerned to hide all the other aspects of his Administration. Mr. Johnson is not merely secretive; he is so committed to misleading the correspondents that James Deakin, who covers the White House for the St. Louis *Post-Dispatch*, has written warningly: "Any politician so clever as to meet himself coming around the corner always finds someone waiting there to remind him where he has been."

So many reporters can now remind Mr. Johnson where he has been that they have eroded his most impressive technique—the one that has been defined as declaring that the brook is too broad for leaping, then leaping it. Originally, Mr. Johnson carried this off with a flourish. He pointed out during his first press conference that President Kennedy's last budget had been $98.8 billion; then, sadly, that about $3.5 billion must be added for "built-in increases"— interest on the national debt and the like—and no one could do anything about it. Thus, the budget must run well over $100 billion. This was dutifully reported as sober fact. Eleven days later, the President announced, "I am working from a budget of $98.8 billion this year. It appears that we will expend about that amount." Then, when the budget was triumphantly submitted to Congress, a miracle —$97.7 billion. And, of course, the President received the fullest measure of praise for frugality and magic. But when he tried to take the correspondents down the same winding road the following year,

having an aide announce that the budget would *have* to be between
$104 billion and $106 billion, they hooted.

Such experiences have persuaded many correspondents that Mr.
Johnson will go to any lengths, in the words of one, "to bend the
Washington press into conformity with his consensus society." Douglas Kiker of the New York *Herald Tribune* has charged that the President "grandly mixes truth, half-truth and non-truth and dares you
to isolate them." Attempting to isolate them by probing elsewhere
is often less than productive; a fact can be made false in an inkling.
When alert correspondents discovered and reported that the President was considering the "Heller Plan" for distributing some Federal
income-tax revenue to the states, Mr. Johnson angrily stopped considering it. Increasingly, sources close to the President are closed off.
The fact that even ebullient Vice President Hubert Humphrey is
under strict control became apparent when he once departed from the
prepared text of a speech, then caught himself with, "I don't know
whether I should have said that or not. That part wasn't cleared."

The extent of Johnson's control did not become fully apparent
until February, 1965. The correspondents had long been frustrated
by the ineffectual twice-daily briefings of Press Secretary George
Reedy (although they sympathize; Reedy must cope with a boss so
abrasive that he sometimes blames his press secretary when editors
fail to play Presidential news on Page One). They began to detect a
new and disturbing note when Reedy would respond sketchily to a
reporter's question and be interrupted by a telephone buzzer. The
correspondents gathered around Reedy's desk could make out what
Columnist Doris Fleeson described as "the imperious tones so familiar to them." Then Reedy would expand confidently on the subject
under discussion—a change that lent what Miss Fleeson called "a
touch of Big Brother Is Watching You."

Each discovery of Johnson's techniques has added to the accu-
mulation of distrust and led the press corps to describe Johnson as
the master of the pseudo-event. When Peter Arnett of AP disclosed
that the United States Information Service had staged a sham battle
in Vietnam for the purpose of making a propaganda movie, one
correspondent said disgustedly, "What can you expect with Johnson

as President?" When, early in 1965, President Charles de Gaulle of France held one of his rare press conferences and President Johnson suddenly called a quickie conference of his own at the same time, many correspondents decided that de Gaulle had been undercut. "Johnson's been around too long to make what he did to de Gaulle an accident," wrote James Marlow of AP. Others, including such respected figures as Arthur Krock of the New York *Times* and Alan Otten of the *Wall Street Journal*, have put into print the general suspicion that Johnson rigs announcements so that he tells all the good news himself and leaves the bad news to his subordinates. "No honest reporter ever leaves a news conference or an interview," Tom Wicker of the New York *Times* has written, "believing he has learned a single fact that the President did not want him to know to begin with."

The result is that President Johnson has become a fast man with an insult. He has called the Washington correspondents "crybabies" and "bellyachers" and, to a friendly columnist, indulged himself in savage caricatures of their behavior during press conferences.

Beginning in April, 1965, when Mr. Johnson had AP and UPI teletype machines installed in his oval office, wire-service editors could expect complaints from the President himself before they were even published. Late on the night of May 13, the UPI machine had hardly finished ticking out a story on the public opening of the President's boyhood home when Pat Sloyan of the UPI Washington Bureau received a call.

"Hello, Pat, this is Lyndon Johnson."

"Yes, Mr. President."

"Say, I have here . . . (pause) . . . A101N from Johnson City, Texas, about the homestead, by Kyle Thompson. Let's see . . . (pause) . . . you say in there that there's going to be a fee for the tour. Well, that's not right at all. The idea is to give it to the people."

"Just a minute, Mr. President, and I'll get the story."

"You see what it says? It says the 'home was opened to the public for fee tours.' That isn't right. You see, it's for free. That's the idea. Do you see that?"

"Yes, Mr. President. It looks like they dropped the 'r' in the word 'free.' I guess they omitted it in transmission."

"Well, Pat, it sure does mean just the opposite of what we mean."

"It sure does, Mr. President. I'll fix it."

"Well, we want it to be free."

"Certainly, Mr. President. I'll straighten it out right away."

"I'd appreciate it if you'd clean this up for me."

"I certainly will, Mr. President."

"We hope you will take the steps necessary to straighten this out."

"Yes, sir, Mr. President."

"Thank you, Pat."

"Thank you for letting us know, Mr. President."

Even if Mr. Johnson eventually abandons his more devious tactics and makes his peace with the press corps, there is reason to doubt that he will ever achieve President Kennedy's success. This is partly because he is not a man who can laugh at himself—he is incapable of personal chagrin—but largely because he views the press as a tool. If the reporters become increasingly antagonistic, the day may come when Mr. Johnson reverts to an attitude that he sometimes expressed when he was Majority Leader: Washington correspondents are hirelings who twist the news to suit the biases of their employers. As Stewart Alsop has written, this is the same as calling a lady a harlot.

CHAPTER NINE

Our Synthetic World

"S.E.G.'s letter of Sept. 7 regarding my remarks about the limited public reaction to Sputnik beautifully illustrates a major point in my paper delivered at the American Psychological Association.

"What I said then was that, in the process of transmitting information from officialdom, through the issue-makers, to the public and back again, there were inevitable distortions growing out of the different perspectives and interests of the transmitters, receivers and information sources.

". . . the reporter, exercising his prerogative of selecting those aspects of my remarks which seemed to him to be of major significance, apparently conveyed to one reader at least, an impression rather at odds with that which I would have preferred. Which . . . only serves to emphasize one of the truly significant problems challenging enlightened democratic processes in an ever more complex world: How can the truly important factors in a situation be selected, transmitted, and responded to so that at each step both the transmitter and receiver know what the other is really talking about?"
—A letter from DONALD N. MICHAEL to the Washington *Post*

Do the Washington correspondents slant their stories to please their employers?

To determine whether the newspaper correspondents of the 1930's were free to report the truth as they saw it, Leo Rosten adopted the novel tactic of asking them. Most of the other political scientists of that time were detached observers in the tradition of Woodrow Wilson, who had thought it perfectly reasonable in his day as an institutional theorist to analyze Congress without ever watching it in action or interviewing Congressmen.

First, Rosten talked with the correspondents and won their confidence. Then he used some of their statements in a questionnaire that all of the correspondents were to fill out anonymously. Among the statements was: "My orders are to be objective, but I *know* how my paper wants stories played." More than 60 per cent of the correspondents answered, "Yes," indicating that they, too, felt subtle pressures designed to make them slant their dispatches in the direction of the publisher's leanings. Another statement ran: "In my experience I've had stories played down, cut or killed for 'policy' reasons." Slightly more than 55 per cent wrote "Yes," a clear indication of blatant pressure. In most cases, the correspondents were bending to the prejudices of Republican-minded publishers. There were hardly any other kind.

This was vivid documentation of a suspicion that had been growing for decades. During the last half of the nineteenth century, newspapers, which had long been the most chaotic of enterprises, had begun to take on the shape and color of big business. Joseph Pulitzer and William Randolph Hearst had emerged as industrial capitalists of the press, and others were emerging. The novelty of this trend was pointed up by Lincoln Steffens. Listening to the shop talk of newspaper executives in 1897, he heard them likening the management of editorial operations to that of department stores and wrote, with a trace of the awe of discovery, "Journalism today is a business."

The obvious links between the new businessmen of journalism and all the other entrepreneurs resulted in a feverish rash of books and magazine articles exposing the press, among them Upton Sinclair's shrill book-length editorial *The Brass Check*. The coolest and most substantive judgment was Will Irwin's series published in *Collier's* in 1911. Among other things, Irwin traced the influence of the commercial milieu on newspapers, showing that a major advertiser would not hesitate to demand wholesale changes in editorial policy and was likely to win at least small concessions: insertions of publicity items for himself and his business and the suppression of damaging news.

The influence of big business was not limited to newspapers. Walter Lippmann, who was an associate editor of *Everybody's Magazine* in 1911, wrote later: "I have seen the inside workings of business pressure. Articles of my own have been suppressed after they were in type." So many other journalists wrote of similar experiences that there was no doubt that the chain of commerce bound the press.

Conspiracy theories grew profusely in the rich environment of exposé. Social critics drew stark word pictures of newspaper and magazine publishers plotting with the other lords of capitalism to subvert mass opinion. Rosten's statistics on the twisting of Washington reportage during the 1930's were the *coup de grâce*, proving that the wellsprings of political information were poisoned at the source.

The conspiracy theories were valuable in that they provided a strong focus on distorted journalism, but an analysis by William Allen White questioned the notion that anything properly describable as a "conspiracy" ever took place. White, a publisher who had made himself and his little Emporia (Kansas) *Gazette* famous through acute insights into American institutions, pointed out that "the publisher associates on terms of equality with the bankers, the merchant princes, the manufacturers and the investment brokers. His friends unconsciously color his opinion. If he lives with them on any kind of social terms in the City Club or the Country Club or the Racquet Club, he must more or less merge his views into the common views of the other capitalists. The publisher is not bought like a chattel. Indeed, he is often able to buy those who are suspected of buying him. But he takes the color of his social environment."

This perspective explains a great deal more than any dark conspiracy theory can—especially the changes in the business world and the simultaneous changes in publishing that have taken place since World War II. For even as the passing of the heavy-handed entrepreneur from the business community and the growth of industrial complexes have led to control by cool business-school graduates, so the demise of the great editorial tyrants and the turbulent economics of the newspaper world have cast up a new breed of publisher.

Some of the old thunderers are still around—powerful, profane men like Eugene Pulliam, who uses his Indiana and Arizona newspapers to pledge allegiance to the nineteenth century almost as though Robert R. McCormick were still living. Pulliam's sense of responsibility is suggested by his instructions to one of his editors: "When people pick up the paper, I want them to say: 'What is that sonuvabitch saying now?' or 'Look what a great guy he is!' " One

Indiana Congressman said resignedly of Pulliam, "I never argue with a man who buys ink by the barrel."

And the political commitment of much of the press is still decidedly Republican. Until 1964, one could have predicted confidently even before the national political conventions that the newspapers which endorsed the Presidential candidates would endorse the Republican, whoever he was, over the Democrat, whoever *he* was, by about $3\frac{1}{2}$ to 1. That was the ratio in 1960, and that had been the average ratio in the preceding seven elections. In 1964, Johnson won the support of more newspapers than Goldwater, 445 to 368. But that was an unusual election in many respects. *Life* and the *Saturday Evening Post*, both of which the Republicans were accustomed to counting on as surely as the dawn, went Democratic. It is impossible to imagine, however, that the lords of the mass media would have supported Johnson had the Republican nominee been William Scranton or George Romney. The nomination in 1968 of a more conventional Republican will undoubtedly lure a majority of the publishers once again.

Nonetheless, the new breed is as different from the Robert R. McCormicks of the past as smooth Henry Ford II is different from cantankerous old Henry I. Most of them are even-tempered businessmen who are more concerned with the balance sheet than with whether liberalism and internationalism are the devil's progeny out of Franklin Roosevelt. Many have become convinced that responsible journalism pays off. The new era is probably epitomized by Samuel Newhouse, who collects Democratic and Republican papers like stamps and cares little where they stand as long as they remain solvent.

Certainly, strong political partisanship has been fading. In the Hoover-Roosevelt election of 1932, only 5.8 per cent of U.S. dailies were independent or neutral. The figure was 5.1 per cent in 1936. During the next five elections, independence and neutrality traced a steep curve: from 13.6 per cent in 1940 to 31 per cent in 1960. The figure was up to 59.5 per cent in 1964, but one wonders whether that was because some publishers were fearful of both candidates.

What these changes of the past three decades mean to the Washington correspondents is apparent in the new answers to the same questions as posed by Leo Rosten in the 1930's. They were asked whether it is still true that "My orders are to be objective, but I *know* how my boss wants stories played." Less than 10 per cent replied "Yes." Asked whether their stories had been played down, cut, or killed for "policy" reasons, slightly more than 7 per cent replied "Yes."

These are slender figures, especially when one considers that there are more than three times as many Democrats as Republicans among the Washington correspondents. About half call themselves "Independents," but it is significant that the newspaper correspondents, like the rest of the press corps, are predominantly liberal. (There is little difference politically between the newspapermen and the other correspondents. There are nearly four times as many Democrats as Republicans among the wire-service and radio-television correspondents, and nearly twice as many Democrats as Republicans among the magazine correspondents.)

The mass media can take little pride in the fact that some correspondents are still coerced into following a party line, but the difference between the 1930's and the 1960's is striking. The basic fairness is suggested by the action on the flagship of the Republican Party, the New York *Herald Tribune*, during the Eisenhower years.

There is no question but that the *Herald Tribune* is *editorially* biased, as a comparison of two editorials makes clear. The first, which appeared in 1951, commented on the fact that Donald Dawson, a high official in the Truman Administration, had accepted twenty-two days of free lodging from the management of a Miami Beach hotel: "Mr. Dawson has very little notion of what is proper and improper. The best proof of that rests on his own story of staying free in a $30-a-day room at the Saxony Hotel. . . . The people expect a high official in the White House to know the difference between proper and improper, and the Saxony episode will be remembered."

The second editorial commented on a similar case involving a Republican, and it took quite a different view of official impropriety.

Sherman Adams, Eisenhower's "assistant President," had allowed a businessman who was benefiting from government contracts to pay more than $2,500 for hotel accommodations Adams used. The *Herald Tribune* editorial in *this* case read: "Whoever knows Sherman Adams knows that he is as honest as the day is long. His personal integrity is as flinty and incorruptible as a piece of New Hampshire granite. Those who are using the Boston hotel bills as an attack upon his character will find such tactics will only boomerang against themselves. The accommodations in question had been rented originally on a continuing basis by a longtime personal friend, Bernard Goldfine."

The decided difference in political outlook between the *Herald Tribune* publisher and those he published were often obvious during the Eisenhower years. Even as *Herald Tribune* editorials were proclaiming the President's vision and triumphs, the paper's columnists were commenting on his myopia and defeats. Walter Lippmann was caustic. In a striking series of columns, Joseph and Stewart Alsop exposed news management under Eisenhower more persuasively than any other correspondents (and followed up with a stinging article in the wholeheartedly Republican *Saturday Evening Post*). In 1960, the *Herald Tribune* plumped for Nixon editorially, but Lippmann and Joseph Alsop (Stewart Alsop had by then become the Washington editor of the *Post*) were emphatically for Kennedy.

As for the reporters in the Washington Bureau, so many of them were so friendly to Kennedy that the Republican National Committee complained, unavailingly, to the *Herald Tribune*'s management. When Washington Bureau Chief Robert Donovan, author of *PT-109*, left to take over the Washington Bureau of the Los Angeles *Times*, the *Herald Tribune* replaced him with David Wise, who had been one of the most effective investigators of Republican wrongdoing.

Perhaps the most persuasive evidence that many political reporters are experiencing a heady new freedom came in 1962. Two leading newspapers announced the establishment of a co-operative news service that would have correspondents employed by each paper cover the world for both, and for any others that were interested in subscribing to the service. Now, each is publishing column after column of reportage from correspondents who work for the other, and more than fifty additional newspapers of varying political persuasions are offering the same fare. One of the founding papers is the ultraliberal Washington *Post*, the other the ultraconservative Los Angeles *Times*.

The uncomfortable minority of correspondents who must bend to pressures from the home office include some who are so sensitive to the fact that their dispatches poison the political dialogue that they suffer through short, unhappy periods of ambivalence, then move on to more congenial bureaus. Others, so well paid that they cannot bring themselves to quit, rationalize their role ("Well, this is a business like any other business") or echo the classic comment of the Chicago *Tribune* reporter who said, "What the hell; morality comes too high." The few correspondents who are controlled from headquarters bend to subtle pressure, not bludgeons. They gradually learn by observing how their stories are processed and displayed—not to mention whether their salaries are increased—that which is prized and that which is taboo.

In some cases, there is no question of bending to pressure; the correspondent's views are a snug fit with his employer's policy. This is true of liberals as well as conservatives, but there is no sharper example than the agreement of Robert E. Baskin, Washington Bureau Chief of the Dallas *Morning News* and *News* Publisher Ted Dealey. The flavor of Baskin's reportage is represented by its contrast with an AP report on the same event:

STUDENT PICKETS MARCH IN CAPITAL

WASHINGTON (AP)—Students picketing for peace marched four abreast in spring-like weather to Arlington National Cemetery Saturday, demonstrating their hopes for disarmament and an end to nuclear testing.

STUDENT MARCH ON CAPITAL TINGED BY BEARDED BEATNIKS

By Robert E. Baskin
Washington Bureau of the *News*

WASHINGTON—Left-wing student peace marchers—with a definite beatnik tinge—marched through the streets of the capital Saturday on a pilgrimage to the Tomb of the Unknown soldier in Arlington National Cemetery.

The value of a Washington correspondent who reflects his employer's attitudes was demonstrated most conclusively, however, late in 1961. An enterprising *News* reporter in Dallas had discovered that the United States was selling Air Force planes to Yugoslavia and training Yugoslav airmen at Perrin Air Force Base in Sherman, Texas. The *News* played the story heavily, as it deserved. Then the Kennedy Administration was damned in a series of "indignation rallies" that fanned out across the country from Texas. The first meeting of the National Indignation Convention in Dallas drew only three hundred people from a city of more than seven hundred thousand. Most editors would have had them venting their indignation on Page Five. But the *News* made the report of the meeting the lead story on Page One.

Among the speakers quoted were Major General Harry Crutcher of the Air National Guard and Air Force Brigadier General William L. Lee. Crutcher advocated a student riot, saying, "Let's learn from the Communists." Lee characterized foreign aid as "the stinkingest, rottenest thing that ever happened to the American people" and said that the mass media "are controlled by traitors." He exhorted the crowd, according to the *News*'s own report, with, "What we want to do is write them Congressmen. We got to clean out the State Department, the CIA and those bureaucracies."

The fact that the local reporter did not polish Lee's language while writing the story may have indicated to some readers that he lacked the spark of indignation that informed the meeting, but no one was left in doubt about the attitude of the editors. An editorial stated: "The *News* is gratified over the patriotism at Memorial Auditorium and hopes that future signs of national weakness will be greeted with the same grassroots objections."

Several days later, however, the Washington *Post* disclosed that the Eisenhower Administration had also been involved. Eisenhower held a press conference. The Associated Press reported that although the deal with Yugoslavia had been completed three days after Kennedy became President, Eisenhower admitted that his State and Defense Departments had approved it, and Eisenhower himself had left Kennedy a memo about it. Significantly, Eisenhower said that the sale of the planes was in "the best interest of the United States."

It was a bad situation for the *News*. Eisenhower was Dealey's, and Dallas's, man. He was clearly implicated in the deal with Communist Yugoslavia, yet the *News* had contributed greatly to whipping up public outrage.

The *News* solved its problem by ignoring the AP story, instead front-paging a report of its own by Baskin under a headline that read: IKE DENIES GIVING OK FOR JETS' SALE. Baskin started his story:

"Who was to blame for the sale of 130 Sabre Jet planes to Communist Yugoslavia—Dwight Eisenhower or John F. Kennedy?

"A controversy over this question mounted in Washington Tuesday.

"Former President Eisenhower, at a press conference in Newark, N.J., asserted flatly Tuesday that the decision to sell the planes was made after he left office.

"He conceded that the sale was discussed by the State and Defense Departments before Kennedy assumed the Presidency, but the final decision was left up to the new Chief Executive.

" 'I did not brief President Kennedy,' Eisenhower said."

There was more to Baskin's story, but nothing more from the Eisenhower press conference. Instead, there was innuendo about the reason for the Washington *Post*'s story ("obviously leaked by the Kennedy Administration"), and anything Texans might consider damaging to Eisenhower was attributed to the liberal *Post*.*

* Here are the AP and *News* reports (the AP report as it was printed in the Austin, Texas, *Statesman*):

IKE HAILS
JETS SALE
TO SLAVS

NEWARK, N.J. (AP)—Former President Dwight D. Eisenhower said Tuesday that he believed the sale of 135 Sabre Jet planes to Yugoslavia "is in the best interest of the United States."

Eisenhower referred to the transaction at a news conference here and in a supplementary statement afterward.

IKE DENIES GIVING
OK FOR JETS' SALE

By Robert E. Baskin
Washington Bureau of the *News*

WASHINGTON—Who was to blame for the sale of 130 Sabre Jet planes to Communist Yugoslavia—Dwight D. Eisenhower or John F. Kennedy?

A controversy over this question mounted in Washington Tuesday.

Former President Eisenhower, at a press conference in Newark, N.J., asserted flatly Tuesday that the decision

It is essential to refute the notion that those correspondents who are under the hand of the home office are controlled primarily

---

The sale was disclosed by the State Department last Friday and drew sharp criticism. The deal includes training eight Yugoslav air force pilots at Perrin Air Force Base, Tex.

Eisenhower said that on December 14, 1960, the Defense Department told the State Department that it had no objection to the sale of the fighter planes, because they were obsolete and headed for a scrap heap.

The State Department approved the sale Jan. 16, the former President said. A release order was issued by the Defense Department Jan. 23, 1961, three days after he left office, Eisenhower said, and the sale was consummated March 10.

In Washington administration sources said Monday that Eisenhower left a memo with President Kennedy outlining reasons for sale of the jets to Yugoslavia.

He said that the United States started its policy of selling non-critical military equipment to Yugoslavia in 1958.

to sell the planes was made after he left office.

He conceded that the sale was discussed by the State and Defense Departments before Kennedy assumed the Presidency, but the final decision was left to the new Chief Executive.

"I did not brief President Kennedy," Eisenhower said, according to a United Press International dispatch.

His denial came on the heels of a story obviously leaked by Kennedy Administration sources saying that Eisenhower had assured Kennedy "that the shipment of surplus F86D Sabre Jets to Yugoslavia was in the national interest."

The Washington Post in its Monday edition quoted an unnamed source as saying that the decision to ship the planes to Marshal Tito was "explained to the incoming President by the outgoing President."

The Post said that Eisenhower had a memo prepared on this and other decisions reached in the final stages of his administration.

Tuesday afternoon Presidential Press Secretary Pierre Salinger stepped into the controversy.

He told reporters he saw no conflict between the Eisenhower statement and what Kennedy Administration officials have said since the row began last week.

No one, Salinger said, had ever reported that Eisenhower had briefed Kennedy on the Yugoslav transaction. Observers noted that this did not clear up the language used in the Washington Post story, which could have come only from Kennedy administration sources.

because publishers have an itch to defeat this program or that political figure. This once happened often, and still happens occasionally, but it is now out of touch with the central reality, which is that home-office ignorance is chiefly to blame. For every correspondent who is bent by his employer's political prejudices, three give in to the fuzzy judgment of editors and publishers who may be two thousand miles from Washington, but who know, by God, how politics works because they were once in Washington or have heard all about the shenanigans at the state capital.

So knowledgeable a publisher as John S. Knight unwittingly revealed not long ago that he is unaware of the basic procedures of Washington reporting. In a biting editorial on State Department information practices, Knight confused "off-the-record" briefings with "background" briefings. Robert Manning, who was then serving as Assistant Secretary of State for Public Affairs, publicly termed this an "amateurish error," pointing out that " 'Off-the-record' means you can't print it, while "background' means you can print it but cannot attribute it by name to the official who said it." Knight further revealed his ignorance of the realities of political reporting by publishing a biting rejoinder: "Yeah, Manning, I know about that. But both practices are vicious in that they either conceal news to which the public is entitled or enable a public official to hide behind statements for which he refuses to take public responsibility." Many correspondents agree that both practices are overused and misused on occasion, but one of Knight's own reporters holds that anonymous briefings and interviews are inevitable. Power relationships in Washington are too complex and unstable to allow every official to speak out boldly on every issue. No correspondent can hope to learn the real truth about controversial issues unless he grants some officials the right to cloak themselves in anonymity. It is often a question of getting the facts from a coy "informed source" or not at all.

Ironically, Knight himself and several other publishers who complain that government officials use "off-the-record" conferences to tie up the Washington press corps were tied up one day by President Kennedy. Knight, Pulliam, Barney Kilgore of the *Wall Street*

Journal, Don Maxwell of the Chicago *Tribune*, and several others—all of whom had opposed President Kennedy—were invited to the White House one day for a two-hour luncheon discussion. When it was over, Washington correspondents were gathered in front of the West Wing door to the White House, waiting to interview the departing guests. Having promised to keep Kennedy's disclosures confidential, the publishers went quietly out the front door. The reporters spotted them. That set up the most ludicrous scene in modern American journalism. To avoid being interviewed, the publishers who are loudest about the need for a free flow of information made a running break for the front gate, with the correspondents in hot pursuit. Several portly laggards who were run down refused to answer questions.

Many of the well-established correspondents have the same status as managing editors and can hold their own in arguments with the home office. One has said: "I've been here so long that there is no conflict of interest between me and St. Louis. I mean St. Louis is influenced just as much by my view as I'm influenced by theirs. I make a hundred decisions where they make one. I'm not bothered by the editorial page; if they take an entirely different viewpoint from mine, that's their affair."

Others, though, as a notable study by Sherry Arnstein reveals, are forever trying to cope with queries and instructions that they consider "lame-brain," "provincial," and "silly." As a consequence, some try to discourage effective communications with editors and publishers. One who was asked what he had done to improve communications with his bosses responded, "Nothing! I like things the the way they are. I would in fact be delighted to hear from them not at all—but that would be a kind of utopia that no Washington correspondent can reasonably expect."

The plight of the younger correspondent is especially acute. Aware that long experience in the hurly-burly of political reporting is greatly prized in journalism, he is usually eager to please the home office and unable to argue points of coverage and emphasis effectively. What sometimes happens is illustrated by the experience of John F. Kennedy on his first assignment. Discharged from the Navy in 1945, he took a job with William Randolph Hearst's International News Service. Since he had lived in England prior to World War II and had written a book on Britain's awkward military stance, young Kennedy was sent to London to report the upcoming elections. One of his first stories predicted that Winston Churchill's Conservatives would lose the elections and control of the British government to Clement Attlee's Labor Party. "No sooner did that story hit New York," Kennedy recalled later, "than I got a rocket from Hearst, practically charging me with being out of my mind. Well, in the next several days I gradually worked it around to where Churchill had rallied and now looked like an easy winner. If I had stuck to my original story, I'd have been a red-hot prophet. As it was, I was just another reporter—wrong."

The Washington correspondent is likely to be, in the phrase with which William S. White describes himself, "pro-politician." The more a correspondent learns about national politics—which is to say, the closer his view of the operations of the federal government —the greater the likelihood that he will respect most of the men and women in public life. Even the self-proclaimed "watchdogs" like Drew Pearson, who dig deep into Washington's subterranea, confess their admiration for those who make the federal establishment work. The correspondent who turns up evidence of corruption is usually aware that corruption is not characteristic of the national political milieu.

In contrast, home-office journalism over much of the United States is characterized by quite another attitude. When Assistant Secretary Manning complained that public officials should not have to accept the kind of abuse John S. Knight lavishes on them, Knight responded derisively: "The rigors of Washington social life must indeed be tough." This is the distinguishing tone of one of the best publishers reflecting on national politics.

Despite his easy access to facts, the provincial editor or publisher may be one of the chief repositories of political nonsense. He is almost certain to be if he reflects a provincial community's attitudes, which, across a great expanse of the United States, spring from distaste for the sophistication of Washington, fear of those who have and use power, and Calvinistic mistrust of the government itself. Thus, it was not at all surprising that an editor who attended a State Department briefing in Washington challenged Secretary of State Dean Rusk to explain why (1) 48,000 cases of Metrecal were sent to India, (2) 300,000 tons of cement were allowed to harden on the docks in monsoon weather in India, and (3) a sugar-beet factory was built in Turkey, where there are no sugar beets. Secretary Rusk delivered a written report: (1) No Metrecal has ever been shipped to India; (2) poorly packaged cement from the *Soviet Union* hardened on the docks in Burma; (3) the United States has never financed a sugar-beet mill in Turkey, but U.S. funds helped construct a mill in Iran that was so successful that two other mills have since been built there.

The wounding fact is that much of the press in handling Washington stories not only reflects community suspicions but feeds and nourishes them as well. It is easy to pardon any of the readers of the San Francisco *News-Call-Bulletin* who may have thought that, two months after the death of John F. Kennedy, his widow had a thing going with Marlon Brando. An Associated Press Wirephoto on the front page showed Mrs. Kennedy and her sister leaving the Jockey Club, "a fashionable Washington restaurant," after dining with Brando and his manager, George Englund. The three-sentence caption, which was headed "JACKIE'S EVENING OUT," ended, "The women left alone, with Brando and Englund departing a few minutes later." Anyone with finely honed suspicions surely read volumes into that.

It is even easier to pardon the suspicious who read the cryptic Associated Press story which accompanied the picture in many other newspapers. The fourth paragraph ran: "An obvious attempt was made to keep the small dinner party from attracting the attention of other guests in the restaurant. . . ."

These reports were factual, in keeping with the tradition of the Associated Press. But how different were the impressions of Washington *Post* subscribers! The caption supplied by the *Post* ended: "The foursome was discussing plans for the second annual Joseph P.

Kennedy International Awards Dinner." The accompanying story, which was written by a *Post* reporter, began: "When Mrs. John F. Kennedy had dinner at the Jockey Club on Monday night, it was for two purposes which both concern the interests of her late husband." Nothing more clearly indicates the need for reporting more than "the facts." The *truth* about the facts is essential.

In San Francisco, in Kansas City, in Washington itself, what we know about public figures and public affairs is largely dependent upon what the mass media tell us. We are always subject to journalism and incapable of doing much about it. We can see too little for ourselves. Days are too short and the world is too big and complex for anyone to be sure of much about the web of government. What most of us think we know is not known at all in the sense of experience and observation.

We get occasional firsthand glimpses by catching an instant's sight of a Presidential candidate in the flesh, by shaking hands with a Senator (or talking with one while he absently shakes hands with someone else), by doing business with the field offices of federal agencies, dickering with the Bureau of Internal Revenue, visiting Washington—all the pitiful little bits and pieces of contact with officialdom that the political scientists describe so grandly as Citizen Participation in Government.

We learn more at secondhand—from friends, acquaintances, and lecturers on hurried tours, especially those who have just come from Washington and are eager to impart what they consider, probably erroneously, to be the real story of what is going on there.

But this is sketchy stuff, and it adds only patches of color to the mosaic. The expanse of our knowledge of contemporary affairs must come from newspapers, radio, television, and magazines. There simply are no practical alternatives. Surely there is a lesson in the fact that the chief psychiatrist for the Federal Bureau of Prisons based much of his analysis of the mental condition of former General Edwin Walker on news reports—and an even better one in the fact that a physician who asked that the psychiatrist be expelled from the

American Medical Association for relying on journalism in so serious a case based *his* request on news reports about the psychiatrist!

Clearly, all of us live in a synthetic world. Our synthesis is fashioned largely from information supplied by the mass media. Yet showing that the mass media provide most of our information is not quite the same as showing that they dictate our opinions. In fact, some thoughtful people doubt that information and opinion are much more than first cousins. Samuel Lubell, one of the most durable of the doorbell-ringers, says: "Most of the voters I talk with are far more biased in their political views than the newspapers they read. Whatever the newspapers do, most voters will continue to shut their eyes and ears to all except what they agree with."

It is true that many of us have unknowingly developed techniques for rejecting, and sometimes reshaping, facts that do not fit our view of the world. We expose our senses primarily to information that reinforces our own ideas. This the psychologists call *selective exposure*. In one test of it, Wilbur Schramm and Richard Carter of Stanford University found that Republicans are almost twice as likely as Democrats to watch a Republican-sponsored telecast. We also tend to see what we want to see—*selective perception*—which social researchers have shown so often that they now have approximately the same compulsion to demonstrate it again that a mathematician has to show that two plus two equals four. Some of us go to ludicrous lengths to perceive "facts" that will support our prejudices. In one experiment, anti-Semites looked at editorial cartoons that ridiculed religious bias and saw them in reverse—as glorifications of Anglo-Saxon lineage. And we unconsciously remember facts that enhance our own views—*selective retention*. Shortly after John Kennedy was elected President, groups of pro-Kennedy college students and groups of anti-Kennedy students were asked to study a highly laudatory article about him. The pro-Kennedy students learned the pro-Kennedy facts sooner and remembered them longer.

Honed to a fine edge by these convenient processes, partisanship can carve out the stuff of rank distortion, all unknown to the person involved. This was clearly the case with a rural Republican who was questioned by a poll-taker during the 1956 Presidential campaign. Although the Republican nominee, President Eisenhower, had had serious medical problems while Democratic Nominee Adlai Stevenson had been enjoying excellent health, the Republican announced his choice with the pride of one who bottoms his preferences on reason: "I'm for Eisenhower; that fellow Stevenson had a heart attack."

Similarly, a scholarly professor used the discussion period following an address by a free-lance journalist to berate a newspaper that had long been the object of his scorn. The professor had read an Associated Press report of a press conference and found it quite different from the account published in the paper. "They took that Associated Press story, changed the headlines, changed some of the words, then published the whole biased business," he said. The journalist said that one part of the charge could not be true because the Associated Press never sends headlines with its news dispatches. It was enough to cause him to check up on the complaint. He found that the paper had not used the Associated Press report at all but had printed an account by its own correspondent—and clearly labeled it with a byline. The professor had been schooled in the apprehensions of scholarly inquiry, but he had allowed his disdain for the paper to color his perception of its report.

But these cases do not prove that facts have no effect on opinion. Some people are almost immune to selecting and shaping facts to fit their biases, and others can be persuaded. There is a case of an introspective woman named Patricia Charney of Washington, who, on the night in October, 1962, when President Kennedy publicly led the nation to the brink of war by announcing on television a quarantine of Cuba, watched in horror and addressed him over and over, "You *fool!* You *fool!*" But then she followed every newscast from that time until noon the following day. "At the end of this vigil," she said, "I found myself in complete agreement with the President's policy." Startled by the change in herself, she asked fifteen acquaintances for their reactions. Six admitted having the same experience.

Public reaction to information is so unpredictable, in fact, that the mass media are continually creating opinion by accident. In

1963 consecutive issues of *Newsweek* recounted one incident in two such different contexts that they created two opposing attitudes. One issue carried a light report in the "Newsmakers" section:

> ... At a seminar for 6,000 students working in Washington for the summer, astronaut John H. Glenn Jr. fielded questions that blasted off in all directions. Those rumors about Glenn running for office—didn't he agree that he isn't qualified to be a senator? The questioner was booed for his impertinence, but Glenn answered cheerily: "You may be right, you may be right."

Casual readers surely concluded that Glenn's modesty and good humor might qualify him for political life. But the same incident was couched in a more serious context in the "Space and the Atom" section of *Newsweek* one issue later:

> But increasingly the extracurricular activities of the astronauts are being questioned. When Glenn faced 6,000 college students in Washington recently, he received rough treatment. Questioned about NASA policies, he replied: "All I know is what I read in the newspapers." Impertinently, one student remarked that if all Glenn knows is what he reads in the papers, then maybe he isn't qualified for the public office he is rumored to want. "You may be right," Glenn conceded.

Upon reading this, an Ohio Democrat who had been touting Glenn for the Senate reflected for publication that the astronaut didn't even seem to be able to handle questions from a bunch of kids.

The influence of information of all kinds is so pervasive that it doesn't even seem to matter that millions of Americans avoid serious reports on public affairs; they are affected in spite of their lack of interest. How this works became clear when a team from the Bureau of Applied Social Research of Columbia University made a full-dress examination of political preferences in Erie County, Ohio. So many people admitted that their votes were often swayed by others that the influentials whose names kept cropping up were labeled "opinion leaders."

It was a sharp breakthrough in social research. Studies of personal influence began to cluster about the theory of opinion leadership, and the leaders in each field were shown to be far more attentive to the mass media than were their followers. In fact, attention to the mass media seems to be a condition of opinion leadership—which is entirely understandable. The unknowing find it difficult to resist the influence of those who can cite pertinent statistics and apt anecdotes. A study of Rovere, New Jersey, shows that those who lead opinion on "cosmopolitan matters"—everything beyond the span of everyday life in Rovere—read news magazines.

When more than one thousand opinion leaders in such fields as business, industry, civic affairs, education, and communications were invited to a White House conference on foreign aid, Professor James Rosenau of Rutgers polled them on a wide range of subjects, including their sources of information. He found that they were chiefly informed by the mass media, especially newspapers and magazines. Seventy-seven per cent relied upon the New York *Times*. The next most influential publication was *Time*.

This much is certain: Our opinions on national affairs begin to take shape with the amalgam of information, opinion, and innuendo which flows to us from Washington through the press corps—an amalgam which has been conditioned at least in part by the predilections of the correspondents, their superiors, government officials, or all three. We are not abjectly at their mercy. Our acceptance, rejection or reshaping is conditioned by the wild array of our own political and psychological leanings—which often means, whether we choose to believe *Newsweek* or *Time*, the New York *Times* or the Los Angeles *Times*, James Reston or David Lawrence, David Brinkley or Fulton Lewis, Jr. Although they usually agree upon what is happening in Washington, they are often at odds as to what it means.

Judged in the light of a theoretical ideal—some visionary notion of machinery that would report and interpret all news of government accurately and dispassionately—this is not a system that seems to deserve prolonged applause. And yet it is almost as idle to try to imagine a different and better system as it is to expect perfection in human affairs. Forty-five years ago, Walter Lippmann traced the troubles of national-affairs journalism and an uninformed democracy to a lack of organized intelligence. He looked to the political scientists to provide it, eventually. The journalist will be able to report news events meaningfully after political science has learned how to supply record and analysis, Lippmann wrote, for then "between him and the raw material of government there will have been interposed a more or less expert intelligence." This was an acute insight into a need, which has been fulfilled in part by adroit reporters, capable of distinguishing between officialdom's selfish ambitions and selfless concerns, and equipped to point them up. In addition, interpretative journalism allows the correspondent more latitude to point to the truth than he was given fifteen years ago, and far more than he had in the 1930's. No longer is national-affairs journalism down with intellectual paralysis: forced by a formula to report the blatant lies of a McCarthy as though they were indelible facts. And no longer is the press corps made up largely of former police reporters who were at home when backroom politics was the focus and lost in a strange land when anything as demanding as elementary economics came to issue. Today, at least a few young specialists are entirely at ease in the arcane reaches of almost anything. "These people," James Reston says proudly, "get *excited* about the Federal Reserve system."

It is nonetheless obvious that the new expertise is a mixed blessing. Mollenhoff may be too caustic in saying that the "watchdogs of democracy have become lapdogs," but his suspicion that some of the specialists are unwitting propagandists for the agencies they cover is close to the mark. Indeed, it would be surprising if a knowledgeable correspondent who covers the Pentagon or the Treasury or the Senate did *not* develop rapport with the knowledgeable officials he sees every day at the grim business of trying to make their part of the government work. If one grants that most government officials are able and patriotic, the wonder would be the correspondent—particularly one who understands defense factors or economics or legislative government—who did not become sympathetic and personally and professionally friendly. In these circumstances, a detached perspective is improbable. Few correspondents are as tough-minded as Reston. Even fewer deserve the accolade one gave Robert Novak: "He has no friends; he just has confederates."

The best solution to the problems suggested here is embodied in the consequences that should flow from an obvious fact: The mass media must face up to their involvement in public affairs.

No informed spokesman denies this involvement. Cost-conscious publishers and broadcasters are likely to interject that a newspaper, a magazine, or a broadcasting station is also a business and must make a profit—but they take pride in work that is tinged with the public interest. "The life-line of democracy" is a familiar phrase in their high councils, and they emphasize their commitment to it by criticizing public officials.

The mystifying part is why they fail to take the natural next step. As Douglass Cater has posited so persuasively, they represent the fourth branch of government—a branch that, however unofficial, needs criticism and the improvement it nurtures quite as decidedly as do the executive, legislative, and judicial branches. The necessity, of course, for the branch that *is* the critic of government, is self-criticism.

There are the beginnings of a self-critical spirit in the incisive judgments of a few journalists, notably Ben Bagdikian, Walter Lippmann, and James Reston. (In a column published a short time before the 1964 political campaigns, Reston urged that newspapers do something about "the dubs and incompetents who represent their states and districts on Capitol Hill," adding, "It would be difficult to overestimate the damage done to the quality of Congress by the amiable good-fellowship of newspaper editors and owners.") There are glimmerings of a new spirit, too, in the fact that the mass media are now quoting other critics as never before—a change that some of the old-timers cannot understand. Shortly before his retirement as Vice-President and Editor of UPI, Earl Johnson wondered in print why newspapers were publishing letters to the editor and editorials critical of AP and his own UPI. "It is odd," he wrote, "that newspapers would pass such views along to their readers about their own two main sources of campaign news."

Judged in terms of the need, however, self-criticism is a languid thing: the news magazines snipe occasionally at newspapers; a few newspapers shoot back; both make scatter-shot surveys of the failings of prime-time television. Only the organs of politics and opinion— *The Reporter, The Nation, The New Republic, Harper's, The Atlantic, Saturday Review, National Review, Human Events* (fugitive publications by the standards of mass journalism)—seem to be consistently concerned. Only *Columbia Journalism Review* and *Nieman Reports* are consistently acute.

What is needed is a critical apparatus. As Walter Lippmann has pointed out, "There are . . . only the first beginnings of the equivalent of bar associations and medical societies which set intellectual and ethical standards for the practice of the profession. Journalism, we might say, is still an under-developed profession."

A model, of sorts, for a critical apparatus that would encourage professionalism exists in the British Press Council. It receives complaints, calls on the responsible editors for explanations, then pronounces judgments. And although it has no ultimate authority—no means of imposing penalties—the Council has succeeded because it has used wisely a weapon the press has reason to respect: publicity. Barry Bingham, the perceptive editor and publisher of the Louisville *Courier-Journal*, has proposed a narrower concept for the United States: local press councils. Bingham would have three to five community leaders sitting as a council to receive complaints, with newspaper executives appearing to present "the journalist's case," and public reports of decisions on television periodically. He is convinced, Bingham told delegates to the annual convention of Sigma Delta Chi, the journalistic fraternity, that "we must put our relations with our readers on a more solid basis of mutual understanding. Such a foundation of public trust is the only permanent protection against censorship, against government control, against any of the other outside influences we dread."

Bingham's plan would be useful for newspapers, most of which

are locally oriented, if newspapermen could only bring themselves
to submit to the criticism of outsiders. (Bingham foresaw this objection and said in his speech to Sigma Delta Chi, "I can hear objections
that a group of laymen could never understand our complicated
problems.") But the existence of the far-flung wire services and the
nation-spanning networks and magazines suggests that a local council, however constituted, would not solve the larger problem. It
would be solved by a proposal offered by Harold Lasswell of Yale
for a national Committee on Public Communication operating much
as the British Press Council does. As a member of the long-dead
Commission on the Freedom of the Press, which was made up entirely of laymen, Lasswell has sad memories of the disdain journalists
showered on the Commission's report. He proposes that the Committee on Public Communication be composed entirely of representatives of the mass media—those, he said, who are "suspected of
integrity." This is a striking suggestion. The mass media, which have
laudable codes aplenty, need now to show that they also have men
of will and vision who can make the codes work.

It is hardly heretical to suggest that a profession seek to purify
itself. Medicine and law have long done so. Even the much-maligned
public-relations practitioners have drawn up a code with teeth and
have expelled from the Public Relations Society of America those
who have not subscribed to it.

It is not enough to say, as some do, that freedom of the press
makes criticisms and codes useless. It is certainly true that no newspaper or magazine can be forced to cease publication, no radio or
television program can be driven off the air by professional outrage.
But the American Association of University Professors has shown
that public condemnation can work remarkable changes in supposedly impregnable institutions. Many a college and university has
been compelled by AAUP censure to change its authoritarian tone.

This is not to say that there should be concerted attacks from the
right on those organs of the left that seem to be drifting toward
"socialism" or attacks on the organs of the right that seem committed
to the restoration of William McKinley. This simply asks that a
reporter, an editor, a publisher, or a broadcaster who abuses the

canons of journalism at least be tested by pitiless publicity to determine whether he is incapable of chagrin.

What, precisely, would the Committee on Public Communication do? It might well study and report on such interesting coincidences as this:

Secretary of Interior Udall has become the symbol of the Kennedy Administration—arrogance coupled with overriding, zealous activity to run roughshod over private interests and spread Government control. He is a prime example of the danger of bestowing too much power on Government agencies. . . . —July 17, 1963, Republican Congressional Committee	Secretary of Interior Stewart L. Udall has become the symbol of the New Frontier Administration—arrogance coupled with overriding, zealous activity to run roughshod over private interests and speed Government control of our lives and properties. He is a prime example of the danger of handing too much power. . . . —July 22, 1963, Item in the Delaware *State News*

The Committee might also consider the larger questions that go to the roots of modern journalism—the kind posed by the reporting of the Kennedy Assassination. Although the mass media have reason to be proud of their work, they should be deeply concerned about the effect of reporting many more facts than there actually were:

Item: The killer's rifle was found by the window on the second floor of the Texas Schoolbook Depository Building. Or it was found in the fifth-floor staircase. Or it was hidden behind boxes and cases on the second floor. Ultimately, all reports agreed that it had been found on the sixth floor.

Item: The rifle was first reported to be a .30-caliber Enfield. Then it was a 7.65 mm. Mauser. But it was also an Army or Japanese rifle of .25 caliber. Finally, it became an Italian-made 6.5 mm. rifle with a telescopic sight.

Item: There were three shots. But some reports mentioned four bullets: one found on the floor of the President's car, one found in the President's stretcher, a third removed from Governor Connally's left thigh, and a fourth removed from the President's body. There was even one report of a fifth bullet. Finally, there was general agreement that there were only three bullets.

So far, the mistakes seem to be of little consequence—small discrepancies fairly quickly resolved. But there is cause for concern when these conflicts of fact are coupled with some of the more mystifying details:

Item: The first reports of the President's wounds described "a bullet in the throat, just below the Adam's apple" and "a massive, gaping wound in the back and on the right side of the head." The position of the President's car at the time of the shooting, seventy-five to one hundred yards beyond the Texas Schoolbook Depository Building, explains the head wound. But how does one account for the bullet in the throat?

Item: The shots were reported to have been fired between 12:30 and 12:31 P.M., Dallas time. It was also reported that Oswald dashed into the house at Oak Cliff where he was renting a room "at about 12:45 P.M." Between the time of the assassination and the time of his arrival at the rooming house, Oswald reportedly (1) hid the rifle, (2) made his way from the sixth floor to the second floor of the building, (3) bought and sipped a Coke (lingering long enough to be seen by the building manager and a policeman), (4) walked four blocks to Lamar Street and boarded a bus, (5) descended from the bus and hailed a taxi, and (6) rode four miles to Oak Cliff. How did he accomplish all this in fourteen minutes?

Item: Oswald was only an "average" marksman in the Marines. A reporter sought out gun experts who were meeting in Maryland at the time of the assassination; they held that, considering the rifle, the distance, the angle, and the movement of the car, "the assassin was either an exceptional marksman or fantastically lucky in placing his shots." The Olympic Champion marksman, Hubert Hammerer, said when he was interviewed in Vienna that *one* shot could have been made under the conditions described, but he considered it unlikely that anyone could have triggered three accurate shots within five seconds with a bolt-action rifle. How did Lee Oswald do it?

As it turned out, these mysteries were not really mysterious. The President's throat wound, it was finally determined, had not been caused by the entry of a bullet but by the exit of a fragment. Oswald had not made his trip in fourteen minutes but in thirty, having arrived at Oak Cliff at about 1.00 P.M. The exceptional marksmanship is best explained by Gertrude Himmelfarb: "But why . . . assume that each of the shots found its intended mark? It would appear that not three out of three but one out of three achieved its purpose (the first inflicting no serious injury and the second hitting Governor Connally). To know how extraordinarily successful or lucky an assassin is, one would have to know how often he was unsuccessful or unlucky." As if to confirm this diagnosis, it was later discovered that Oswald had tried and failed to kill General Edwin Walker.

Now it is easy to pardon the mass media for this confusing array of facts. The *news* of the assassination was drawn almost entirely from authorities. After all, reporters did not say that a bullet entered the President's throat; they quoted Drs. Malcolm Perry and Kemp Clark of the Parkland Memorial Hospital in Dallas, who turned out to be wrong. The Dallas Police first identified the rifle as a .30-caliber Enfield and a 7.65 mm. Mauser. A Secret Service man said he thought the weapon was a .25-caliber Army or Japanese rifle. The housekeeper at the Oak Cliff rooming house said that Oswald had come dashing in at about 12:45. And so on.

For a reporter to quote others rather than making statements on his own authority is in the best tradition of journalism. But the central question is whether that tradition is good enough. Should reporting be democratic to the point that everything posing as fact has equal status? It is one thing to state certainties—the President has been shot and is dead—and quite another to quote a seeming authority—the nearest Secret Service man, a flustered housekeeper— whose speculations breed suspicion.

And suspicion is the point. When "facts" are published, then withdrawn and replaced with other "facts," the whole exercise has the appearance of authorities bringing inconvenient details into line with indisputable evidence—a conspiracy to mislead. Given a mass of conflicting and mystifying details about the actions of an accused assassin, one naturally looks for an easier explanation. Perhaps Oswald was not the assassin—except that so many of his actions point that way. Perhaps, then, he had an accomplice; "No one remembered for sure seeing Ruby between 12:15 and 12:45," wrote one reporter (who could not have interviewed *everyone*)—and the reader's mind leaps to the desired assumption. No wonder the bookstores have been heavy with such volumes as *Who Killed Kennedy?* and *Who* Really *Killed Kennedy?*

It should, then, be part of the mission of the Committee on Public Communication to weigh and explore the effects of journalistic tradition—and especially to determine whether the proud Age of Instant Communication might not be better served if it were not so dedicated to speed.

All this should not suggest that the Committee would be only a negative force. The mass media are met with increasing attacks, many of them ill-informed and uninformed, and the scattershot defenses offered by self-appointed spokesmen are increasingly useless. What is needed is an authoritative body which gains from its criticisms of the media the position and respect that will enable its defenses to be heard and heeded.

Thus, a Committee which praises as well as damns, which defends as vigorously as it attacks. A Committee following such a policy could shine a searing light on those components of the mass media which, in Alan Barth's shrewd phrase, were started by men who had something to say but are carried on by men who have something to sell. A Committee with such a policy could focus public attention on the altogether unsung *Congressional Quarterly* and *Editorial Research Reports*, journalistic enterprises both—and both of which have lent substance and value to journalism, to political science, and to the practice of politics itself.

Such a policy might rid the Washington press corps of those correspondents whose distinguishing characteristic is their questionable choice of vocation—the ones who have stumbled to the conclusion that journalism is a "game." Such a policy would establish a firmer footing for the correspondents who now work in the best tradition of the responsible reporter. Fortunately, their numbers have increased; and their seriousness and purpose are reflected in Lippmann's changing opinion. He no longer laments, as he did in the 1920's, that journalism is only a refuge for the vaguely talented.

Index